£1-50
8/1

MANAGING PROBLEM BEHAVIOURS

A practical guide for parents and teachers of young children with special needs

Susan Dodd

BA DipEd MEd

Co-ordinator, Early Intervention Service,
Autistic Association of NSW

Illustrated by Joanna Davies

WEST SU
MID-SUS
JUNCTIO
BURGESS
SUS
0444-243150

GW00690121

108

MACLENNAN + PETTY
SYDNEY • PHILADELPHIA • LONDON

First published 1994

MacLennan & Petty Pty Limited
80 Reserve Road, Artarmon, NSW 2064 Australia
© 1994 MacLennan & Petty Pty Limited

All rights reserved including that of translation into
other languages. No part of this book may be reproduced
or transmitted in any form or by any means, electronic
or mechanical, including photocopying, recording, or any
information storage and retrieval system,
without permission in writing from the publishers.

Copying for Educational Purposes
Where copies of part or the whole of this book are made
under section 53B or section 53D of the Act, the
law requires that records of such copying be kept and the
copyright owner is entitled to claim payments.

National Library of Australia
Cataloguing-in-Publication data:

Dodd, Susan M.
Managing Problem Behaviours: A practical guide for
parents and teachers of young children with special needs

Bibliography.
Includes index.

ISBN 0 86433 096 0

1. Behavior disorders in children. 2. Developmentally
disabled children. 3. Developmentally disabled children—
Education (Preschool). I. Title.

362.4048

Printed and bound in Australia

Acknowledgements

To Clare, Deirdre, Fran, Libby, Michelle and Row, your support, encouragement and, most importantly, your ideas and contributions are gratefully acknowledged.

To Jacqui in appreciation of your valuable comments and insights on an early draft.

To Sharon Apolony, a special thank you, because without your assistance, this book would never have progressed past the initial, very rough draft.

Contents

Introduction

This guide to managing problem behaviours in young children was written after many requests for help and information by parents and preschools. It is designed to inspire and suggest ideas to parents and other carers who have to deal with extremes of behaviour in young, special needs children. It is not meant to be, and cannot be, a solution to all behaviour problems: there is no easy answer that will work in every situation. The aim is to provide a starting point to encourage parents to look at their own child; to begin to understand why specific problem behaviours may occur and to initiate strategies to manage such behaviours.

Traditional approaches to behaviour management were not very successful when applied to the problem of disabled children. Current trends are also based on behavioural principles, but the focus has shifted away from eliminating or suppressing the behaviour to looking at the cause or function of the problem behaviour, and teaching more appropriate or effective alternative responses.

To change problem behaviours, we must look beyond the actual behaviour itself to the wider environment—what was happening before the behaviour occurred; what happened after the behaviour (what reaction did the behaviour achieve); what message was the child attempting to convey through the behaviour; what were the external factors that provoked the particular behaviour? The problem behaviour may be either an intentional or an unintentional message from the child. An intentional message may be some form of tantrum behaviour that allows the child to avoid an unwanted situation. An unintentional message is one that *we* interpret; for example, a child may self-stimulate (such as rocking) because he is bored or is not being stimulated in any other way.

Some of the myths and misconceptions about the sources and solutions of problem behaviour must be dispelled! Parents should be encouraged to confidently tackle these behaviours that so often disrupt the family and interfere with their child's ability to learn. This guide discusses the need to look at problem behaviours in a broader context, and provides examples of such behaviours and possible solutions for dealing with them. Some of the unhelpful fallacies that have often been suggested are put to rest.

Part A looks beyond behaviour-management programs for young, special needs children. What is problem behaviour? When does it occur? How should problem behaviour be approached? What is the best way to tackle a given problem? Most importantly, why does problem behaviour occur?

In Part B, behaviour-management procedures are considered. There are many things that can be done when the problem behaviour has been identified.

In Part C, a number of common problem behaviours and some strategies that work are identified.

Part D describes and discusses management strategies for certain behaviours that are difficult to control with usual approaches.

Finally, this guide provides a glossary of important terms that may be encountered in reading and in discussions with teachers, medical staff and other parents. This can be used as a ready reference.

PART A:
Defining Problem Behaviour

Chapter 1

What Is Problem Behaviour?

"Behaviour is often children's alternative to language—their loudest voice."

Baker et al. (1976)

Problem behaviour is usually thought to serve no useful purpose. Tantrums, aggression, self-injury, self-isolation and refusal to comply seem to be extreme behaviours that are strange and sometimes downright bizarre. However, we have learned from recent research that most problem behaviours occur for a reason. We must look for the message in the behaviour in each situation; that is, what is the child trying to convey through the behaviour? A child who is kicking, screaming or biting is communicating some message. Attempts to deal with these behaviours in isolation will often miss the point of the message being conveyed.

Stancliffe (1989) described problem behaviour as "the most effective means a person with poor communication skills has of exerting some control over a particular situation". A child uses behaviour to communicate wants and needs; to get a message across to others about how she is feeling, what she wants changed in her surrounding environment; or as a way of coping with frustrations encountered in her day-to-day life. Most of us try to organise our world to avoid uncomfortable, embarrassing or confusing situations. A child with special needs is no different, and tries to modify her world to suit her needs. The problem behaviours are often motivated by such efforts.

Some problem behaviours are more obvious and some are more severe in different situations. For example, if a child is hitting out, screaming, throwing objects or being non-compliant, there will be stress and anxiety placed upon both herself and those around her. Some children, however, display more subtle behaviours, such as self-stimulation, crying when left alone, playing obsessively or wandering aimlessly. These behaviours may not be as disruptive to family life, but they are just as significant and cause anxiety to those caring for the child.

There are different types of behavioural problems:

1 Behaviours that directly interfere with a child's ability to learn and to process information. For example:
   - self-stimulatory behaviours such as rocking and flapping;
   - severe tantrum behaviours
   - obsessive behaviours such as lining up objects or following particular rituals.

2 Behaviours that prevent a child from using skills that she has already learned. For example:
   - refusing to dress, use the toilet, or feed herself;
   - refusing to participate in some play activities.

3 Behaviours that disrupt the family and may cause harm to the child. For example:
   - aggression against others;
   - self-injurious and tantrum behaviours such as head-banging and hand-biting;
   - poor sleeping habits.

Most behaviours fall into more than one of these categories. For example, tantrum behaviours prevent the child from learning and also disrupt the family; self-stimulating behaviour prevents the child from learning and also from using skills already acquired; and self-injurious behaviour may prevent the child from using skills, disrupt the family and may cause harm to the child.

"The circumstances surrounding the behaviour and its purpose are vital ingredients in understanding the behaviour."

Stancliffe (1989)

To understand why problem behaviour occurs and how to deal with it effectively, we must look at what happens before the behaviour and also the changes that occur in the child's environment as a direct result of the behaviour. Behaviour does not occur in isolation and we need to know as much as possible about the context or situation rather than just the behaviour itself. It is essential to determine what function the behaviour serves for the child, and to determine what variables are influencing the child to behave in a certain way. This should then allow us to determine why the problem behaviour occurs.

By recalling what happened to the child immediately before the behaviour (the antecedents) and noting what follows (the consequences), we are able to gain some insight into why particular behaviours occur. The consequences of problem behaviours also allow us to predict if a particular behaviour is likely to occur again, that is, if the behaviour allows the child to avoid a task, then we can expect that such behaviour will occur next time the task is required.

If we understand when and why particular problem behaviours occur, and what the child obtains from the behaviour, we are more likely to be successful in managing these behaviours in a systematic way.

For example, Billy refuses to go to bed at night. He screams and has tantrums when put into his room, and so, to calm him, his parents allow him to come out to sit with them and watch TV.

This may be explained as follows:

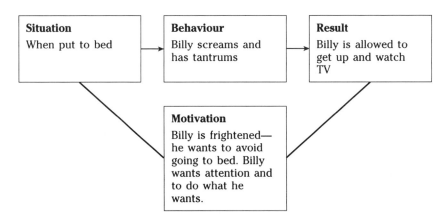

By looking beyond the problem behaviours, we are able to gather more information that will help us to understand why certain behaviours occur, and also help us to develop some management strategies to modify the behaviours. From the example above, we know that the problem behaviour occurs when Billy has to go to bed. The problem behaviour usually results in Billy being allowed to sit up and watch TV. The motivation behind the behaviour may

include avoiding an unwanted event, achieving something he wants to do and also to focus attention on himself. It is also possible that Billy may be frightened in his room. Whatever the situation, it is important to look closely at what is happening when the behaviour occurs, so that we can respond positively and constructively to the message that the child is attempting to convey.

In order to encourage more appropriate behaviour from Billy at bedtime, it is necessary to understand his motivation and to look at alternative and appropriate ways of allowing him to achieve this. An alternative bedtime sequence could therefore be encouraged:

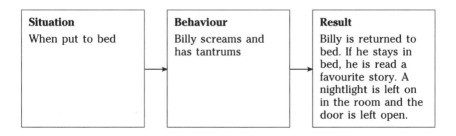

Situation	Behaviour	Result
When put to bed	Billy screams and has tantrums	Billy is returned to bed. If he stays in bed, he is read a favourite story. A nightlight is left on in the room and the door is left open.

Once Billy realises that screaming and crying do not achieve his objective, and he is given a pleasant alternative to staying up and watching TV, he is more likely to remain in bed in future. He is still obtaining attention and bedtime becomes a pleasant experience.

No two children are alike. Each child has her own way of doing some things, not doing others and using her own unique style. Yet, there are useful ways to look at, understand and change problem behaviour, no matter how different the child or how challenging the behaviour.

To change inappropriate behaviour, we must look beyond the behaviour to the context in which it takes place—when it happened will help us to understand why it happened.

Chapter 2

When Does Problem Behaviour Occur?: Situation

Before we are able to design a specific management program, we need to look carefully at when a problem behaviour tends to occur. We will often discover information that will help us to explain why it occurs and thus give us a better insight into the problem behaviour itself.

For example, Billy refuses to sit at the table and eat dinner. He runs around the room and continually has to be brought back to the table.

After careful observation, Billy's mother notices that his behaviour is only a problem at dinnertime. He sits and eats his meal with her at breakfast and lunch quite happily. It is then discovered that Billy's behaviour is a problem at mealtimes when his father is present. Obviously, Billy is no longer the focus of attention at dinner, and so has discovered a way of forcing his mother and father to focus on him and not on each other. In this instance, Billy's problem was rewarded by attention. By looking beyond the behaviour itself to when it occurred and also what happened after, Billy's parents began to get some ideas on how to change Billy's behaviour.

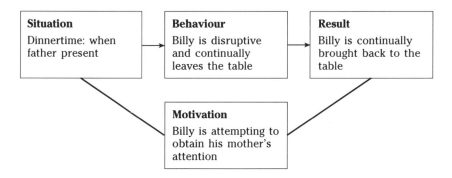

In this example, it is extremely important to identify exactly when the problem behaviour occurs. This allows us to then discover Billy's motivation for behaving inappropriately at dinnertime. Once we understand Billy's motivation for being disruptive during dinner, we can then implement some changes to the evening meal to encourage more appropriate behaviour.

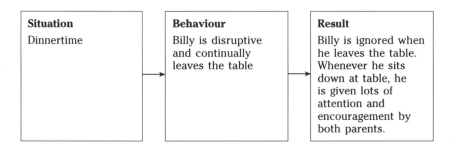

As soon as Billy realises that he wins attention by remaining seated at the table, he is less likely to jump up and run around the room. It is important to remember that Billy's behaviour in this situation may initially become worse before it begins to improve. If Billy has previously achieved his objective through inappropriate behaviour, he is not likely to give up on this method without a fight.

Another example that illustrates the importance of understanding how the situation can affect a child's behaviour is the following. Billy is happy at home and usually plays quietly by himself. Whenever Billy's mother takes him shopping, Billy becomes extremely agitated and screams and cries, especially in the large supermarket.

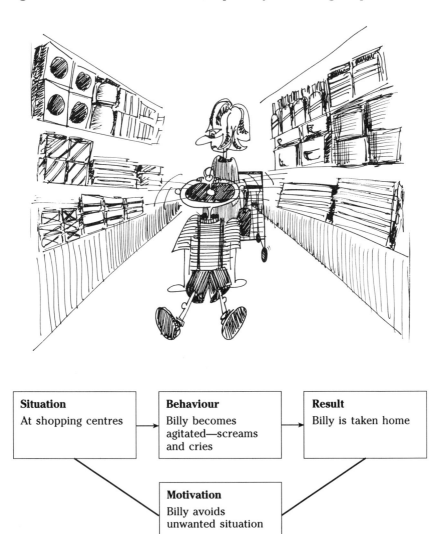

Situation	Behaviour	Result
At shopping centres	Billy becomes agitated—screams and cries	Billy is taken home

Motivation
Billy avoids unwanted situation

From this information, one possible assumption is that Billy has difficulty coping in large, unfamiliar and overwhelming settings. He uses inappropriate screaming and crying to communicate his fear and stress and also to avoid the unwanted situation.

From the information gathered by looking beyond the problem behaviour to the situation, result and motivation, we can once again modify events to achieve more appropriate behaviour. In this example, if Billy's behaviour is an attempt to avoid an unwanted or stressful situation, to help Billy to overcome his fears and stress, it may be necessary to modify the situation by avoiding large, noisy shopping centres. Billy should be introduced gradually to these unfamiliar settings by taking him initially to smaller, quiet and less crowded centres; telling him beforehand exactly where he is going, what he will be doing and also stressing that he will return home immediately afterwards.

Billy is given information to help him cope in the unfamiliar and unwanted situation. A further incentive would be to ensure that there is something pleasant or rewarding for Billy—either a ride, an ice cream or a small visit to the park on the way home.

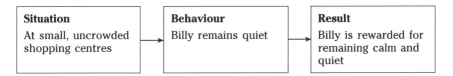

Situation	Behaviour	Result
At small, uncrowded shopping centres	Billy remains quiet	Billy is rewarded for remaining calm and quiet

It is not always immediately possible to understand a child's motivation, or the function of a problem behaviour in a given context, without first testing a number of possibilities. The behaviour may be an intentional or an unintentional message that may require interpretation to determine what the child is trying to convey.

Once we understand the importance of looking at the situation that precedes problem behaviour, and the motivation for the behaviour, we can design and implement strategies to modify the behaviour. We can use the information obtained to modify the situation and encourage more appropriate and acceptable behaviours. The information will allow us to formulate ways of preventing further incidents of problem behaviour through education and management of the child.

The information obtained by studying the situation immediately preceding problem behaviour may be used to decrease the likelihood of the behaviour occurring again. It gives a clear picture that is useful in determining why the behaviour is occurring, that is, what is the function of the behaviour for the child in a particular context.

Chapter 3

What Happens after Problem Behaviour?: Result

> 1 Behaviours followed by positive consequences are more likely to happen again.
> 2 Behaviours that are not followed by positive consequences are less likely to happen again.

A child's behaviour is usually determined by the expected results of her actions. She is usually motivated to behave in a certain way by the rewards she expects to receive from that behaviour. A child learns to behave in a way that leads to events or actions that are pleasing for her. A child also learns to avoid situations which she finds unpleasant or non-rewarding.

For example, Billy always bites or hits other children to avoid having to share.

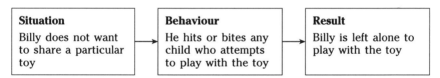

Situation	Behaviour	Result
Billy does not want to share a particular toy	He hits or bites any child who attempts to play with the toy	Billy is left alone to play with the toy

The result of Billy's aggression is that the other children leave him alone and no longer attempt to share the toy. Because the problem behaviour is immediately followed by a positive result, it is safe to assume that Billy's aggression is likely to continue to occur. A better result would have been to remove the toy from Billy for two minutes and give attention to the bitten child.

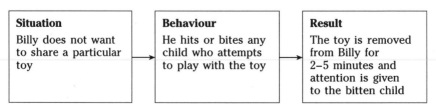

Situation	Behaviour	Result
Billy does not want to share a particular toy	He hits or bites any child who attempts to play with the toy	The toy is removed from Billy for 2–5 minutes and attention is given to the bitten child

Billy is not only denied access to the toy, he is also ignored. Since the behaviour is not followed by a positive consequence, it is less likely to happen again.

In another example, Mary always pushes her brother away if he ever tries to share or play with her toys.

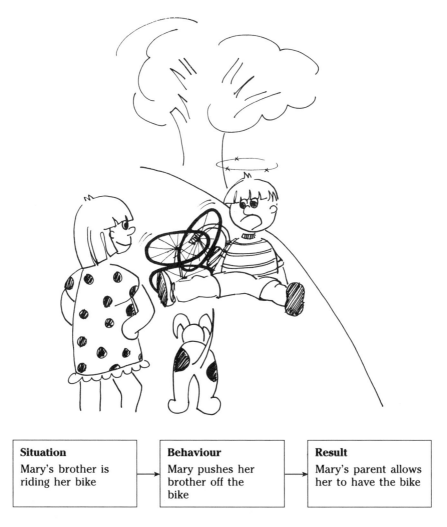

Situation	Behaviour	Result
Mary's brother is riding her bike	Mary pushes her brother off the bike	Mary's parent allows her to have the bike

The positive consequence for Mary from her aggression is that she is allowed to have her bike back, and so her aggression is rewarded. Because her problem behaviour is immediately followed by a positive consequence, it will probably be repeated next time her brother is riding the bike. A much better response to the aggressive behaviour would have been to deny Mary access to the bike and also to ignore her.

Situation	Behaviour	Result
Mary's brother is riding her bike	Mary pushes her brother off the bike	Mary's parent/carer takes away the bike and locks it in the shed. Mary is ignored and attention is given to her brother.

Mary is not only denied access to the bike, but also she is ignored. Since her behaviour is not followed by any positive consequence, it is unlikely that it will occur again.

In these two examples, it is important to look not only at the immediate consequences of the children's behaviour, but also to understand the possible motivation behind their actions. The immediate behaviour-management strategy may be to ensure that there is no positive consequence for the children from the particular behaviour, but at the same time, it is also essential to implement some longer-term goals or objectives to provide Billy and Mary with skills to be able to share, to play appropriately and to tolerate other children within their immediate "space". Billy and Mary could be taught some additional strategies such as turn-taking under adult supervision, alternative ways of communicating and accepting contingent reinforcement for appropriate behaviour. Contingent reinforcement is reinforcement that depends upon a specific response. For example, Billy takes turns with another child for a toy for five minutes, the other child is then removed, and Billy is rewarded by being allowed to play with the toy on his own. Billy and Mary will eventually learn some new skills that will allow them to attain what they want in a more acceptable way.

In order to achieve positive results from any behaviour-management program, it is necessary to look carefully at what the child achieves through her behaviour. It is important to understand the child and her particular disability, and to look for all possible motivations that may require not only immediate behaviour-management strategies but also longer-term programs to help the child develop some necessary skills. It is important to discourage problem behaviours, but also to encourage alternative behaviours so that the child is able to achieve her wants or needs.

Chapter 4
Why Does Problem Behaviour Occur?: Motivation

A child with limited communication skills often uses behaviour to exert some control over a particular situation. Behaviour problems increase when a child is bored, confused, anxious or frustrated or when the child does not have alternative or more functional ways to behave. Traditional behavioural approaches focussed on eliminating problem behaviours that were often the child's only way of communicating. They did not provide the child with any alternative skills to replace the problem behaviour.

In order to deal successfully with problem behaviour, it is necessary to know and understand the child—to learn to read the child's communicative messages before he becomes totally frustrated, and to teach him other, more efficient ways to send messages. Many behaviour problems may be prevented by adjusting the child's environment, modifying his routines and activities, and simplifying our communications with the child and our expectations of him.

Problem behaviour is often a result of one of the following motivations: avoidance; attention-seeking; "I want"; self-stimulation.

1 Avoidance

- Problem behaviour can serve as a means to escape or avoid unpleasant situations.
- The message is as if to say, "I don't want to do this."

Consider the following: in the afternoons, when her mother tries to teach Mary, Mary cries and her mother gives up trying to teach her.

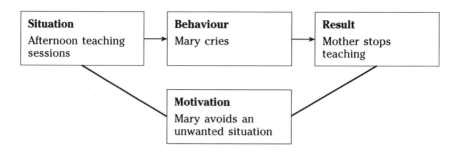

Situation		Behaviour		Result
Afternoon teaching sessions	→	Mary cries	→	Mother stops teaching

Motivation
Mary avoids an unwanted situation

Avoiding an unwanted situation is very rewarding. A lot of problem behaviour is rewarded by allowing a child to escape or avoid unwanted situations. These situations often occur when unfamiliar or unwanted demands are placed upon the child (for example, a new teaching activity) or during activities that the child does not like (for example, bedtime, shopping).

Many children learn that a well-timed tantrum will avoid a situation or at least postpone it. For example, Billy refuses to clean his teeth.

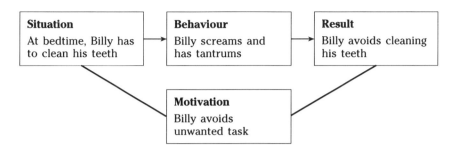

Billy successfully avoids cleaning his teeth by screaming and crying.

2 Attention-seeking

- Positive social reinforcement, such as praise, can motivate some problem behaviours. The attention need not always be pleasant to be positively reinforcing. Even negative attention, such as an angry look, can be better than no attention.
- The message is, "Pay attention to me."

As an illustration: at dinnertime, his parents are talking to each other and Billy jumps up from the table. Billy then gets attention from family members chasing after him.

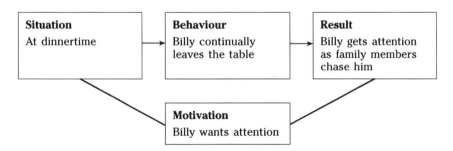

Attention-seeking offers a powerful motivation for problem behaviour. All children seek attention, and many special needs children do not differentiate between positive and negative attention. To some children, attention such as scolding, shouting or chasing is often just as rewarding as praise, hugs and smiles. Even simply looking at a child may be rewarding.

For example,

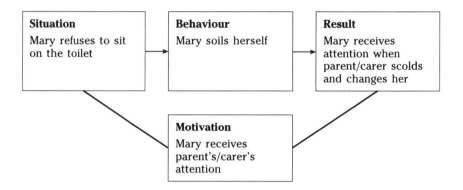

Mary has learned to obtain her parent's/carer's attention, and will continue to refuse to sit on the toilet and will soil herself while the attention is provided.

3   "I Want" Behaviour

- The purpose of such behaviour is to get some object or activity.
- Some children may be aggressive in trying to get things they want (attacking the child who has an object, grabbing, screaming, etc.).

Sometimes when a child screams, we assume that he wants something, especially when mere attention does not calm him. Usually we feed him, or give him something that we think he likes.

As children develop, they are usually able to express their wants or needs verbally or satisfy them independently. For some children, however, the ability to say or do or wait develops more slowly, and often to a more limited degree. Some children find it easier to express their needs and desires through behaviour. Parents will often unknowingly reinforce this "I want" behaviour by continuing to reward the inappropriate behaviour. Objects or activities that the child desires might either be given to him if he has tantrums, or promised to him if he will be quiet.

For example, at preschool when Billy wants a certain toy, he will hit, kick or bite the child with the toy to obtain it.

Situation	Behaviour	Result
At kindy, a child is playing with blocks	Billy kicks the child with the blocks	Billy is given the blocks to keep him quiet

Motivation
Billy gets what he wants

The teacher has reinforced Billy's aggressive behaviour against another child to keep Billy happy and quiet.

4 Self-stimulating Behaviour

> - These behaviours seem to be enjoyable and thus reinforcing for their own sake.
> - Often the behaviour seems unrelated to the behaviour of others, as it often continues for long periods regardless of whether or not others are present.

It is not always possible to be sure of the child's motivation for behaving in a certain way—sometimes we can only guess and may be wrong. That is why it is so important to gather as much information as possible about a target behaviour before implementing any specific behaviour-management program.

As an illustration: at home during the day, Mary continually rocks back and forth. Mary's possible motivation for her self-stimulatory behaviour may include avoiding contact with other people, providing some stimulation for herself to reduce boredom, creating some sense of order and structure in uncomfortable or unfamiliar situations, or for entertainment.

We need to focus not only on the actual problem behaviour, but also on the context in which it occurs and the function or meaning of the behaviour for the child.

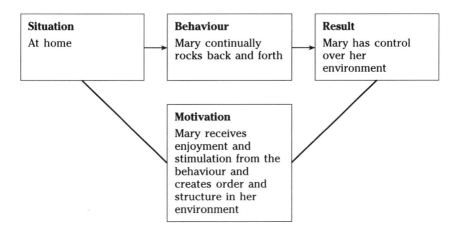

Self-stimulating behaviours, fearful behaviours, obsessive behaviours or self-injurious behaviours are discussed in more detail in Part D.

Why does the child need to behave inappropriately to receive attention? Why does the child use behaviour to obtain wants and needs, and why does a child want to self-stimulate? Once we have possible answers to some of these questions, we are more able to provide assistance to teach relevant skills, and structure the environment to give the child ways to behave more appropriately.

It is important to recognise and understand that there are several possible motivations underlying specific problem behaviours used by children to achieve their particular wants and needs. Teach children new skills or restructure the environment so that the need for such behaviour is reduced or eliminated.

Chapter 5

Setting up a Behaviour-management Program

In order to develop strategies to change or manage a particular problem behaviour, it is important to understand clearly the techniques to follow in setting up a program. There are no magic answers or secret remedies to make a child behave appropriately. There are, however, some techniques that will help to teach a child more acceptable behaviour. It is important that the people who are most involved with the young child—parents and preschool teachers—have the skills and knowledge to implement behaviour-management techniques. After all, they are the people who know the child, spend most time with her and decide what is best for her.

When trying to understand what motivates a child to behave in a certain way, an important rule to remember is that later behaviours are determined by what is first achieved by a particular behaviour. Once this rule is understood, parents and carers may be able to view behaviour from a different perspective.

For example, Billy enjoys playing with his toys more and will play quietly for longer periods, because his parents pay attention to him when he is playing quietly.

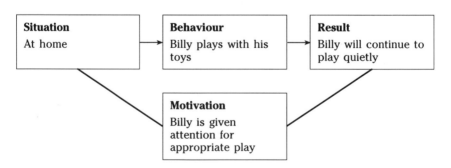

Because Billy is given attention for appropriate play, and this is something that Billy enjoys, he is more likely to continue to behave in such a way in the future.

There are a number of steps to follow in initially setting up a behaviour-management program. These are:

1 Describe precisely and specify the behaviour to be changed, that is, **select a target behaviour.**

2 Choose a method of recording relevant information about the target behaviour, that is, **observe and measure the behaviour.**

3 Record and measure the behaviour in the situations where it normally occurs, that is, **collect a baseline.**

4 Identify the behaviour pattern, that is, what is usually happening before the behaviour occurs and also what happens as a result of the behaviour. Try to understand the child's motivation for the problem behaviour.

1 Describe the Behaviour

The very first step is to decide exactly what behaviours are to be changed. Some behaviours should be modified so that they occur less often, while others should occur more often. For example, Billy should be encouraged to scream or hit other children less often, but should also be encouraged to dress and toilet himself more often. The behaviours that are selected for change are called **target behaviours**.

A target behaviour is one that needs to be changed, to occur more or less often.

In order to change or modify a child's behaviour, we have to identify it specifically. General descriptions and labels such as hyperactive, aggressive, withdrawn do not provide enough information about the problem behaviour to allow us to develop management strategies. For example, it is of little use to define the behaviour as: "Billy has temper tantrums." It is much more informative to describe the behaviour precisely and in more detail: "Billy screams, bangs his head and drops to the floor when he is in a one-to-one teaching session." This description gives specific information about the problem behaviour rather than a general observation. The information includes details of the child's reaction, as well as describing when the problem behaviour actually occurs. From a specific description of the problem behaviour, it is possible to determine what should be observed and measured.

A target behaviour must be clearly defined in objective and measurable terms in order to know when it is occurring, but also so that it can be measured accurately. For example, "Billy has poor eating habits" should be more clearly defined to give specific information, such as, "Billy throws his food and spits it onto the floor, and refuses to sit at the table during meal times."

Whenever we select a target behaviour to modify, it is also important to think of a few related but more appropriate behaviours to focus on at the same time. The aim is to encourage the child to engage in these more appropriate behaviours rather than the target behaviour. As the child is unable to behave appropriately and inappropriately at the same time, the focus should be on increasing the acceptable behaviours to allow the child less time to engage in the inappropriate target behaviour.

> Whenever we select a target behaviour to decrease, we should always select several appropriate behaviours to increase.

For example, Billy's unacceptable mealtime behaviours of spitting and throwing food may be paired with appropriate mealtime behaviours of chewing and swallowing food, using a fork and spoon, and sitting quietly at the table.

Summary

The first step in setting up a program to manage problem behaviour is to select the target behaviour carefully. The target behaviour is one that needs to be changed or modified. Once the target behaviour has been chosen, it should be defined precisely so that it is observable and measurable.

At the same time as selecting the target behaviour to be changed, choose a number of appropriate behaviours to be increased. These behaviours should be incompatible with the target behaviour.

Finally, choose only target behaviours that are important to both parents and the child.

The following sample sheet may help you to understand and carry out the initial step of selecting the target behaviour and defining it precisely.

Sample Sheet

a) *Define the Target Behaviour*
Define the target behaviours below in observable, measurable terms.

Target Behaviour	Definition
Billy is aggressive	Billy hits and bites his sister whenever she tries to touch him or play with his toys
Billy won't go to bed	
Mary is disruptive	

b) *Select Alternative, Appropriate Behaviours*
Select several appropriate behaviours that are incompatible with the target behaviours listed below.

Target Behaviour	Appropriate Behaviour
Screaming	Playing quietly, pointing to desired objects, taking turns, waiting and requesting verbally and non-verbally.
Biting	
Wetting pants	

2   Observe and Measure the Behaviour

Observation and data collection are an important part of any program designed to deal with problem behaviours. Our understanding of behaviour is enhanced by careful observation of the behaviour in the situations it normally occurs.

There are different approaches to recording relevant information. Each approach has its advantages and disadvantages, but the one that is most appropriate will depend on the actual behaviour targeted for change, the time available for recording and the frequency of occurrence.

One way to record information about a specific target behaviour is to **record throughout the day**. This means that the behaviour is observed and recorded every time that it occurs throughout the day and night. This method of recording information is usually the best method to use for behaviour that does not occur frequently.

If the target behaviour occurs frequently throughout the day, it can be very time consuming to observe and record each occurrence, so it may be more viable to record information for only part of each day.

A second way of recording information is to **record for a specific period during the day**. This means that every occurrence of the behaviour is recorded during stipulated periods of the day. This approach is usually effective for behaviours that occur only at certain times during the day (for example, mealtimes, bedtime).

A third approach is to **check and record briefly at different times during the day** to see if the child is engaged in the specified target behaviour. This method is used when the behaviour occurs almost continuously throughout the day and you do not want to spend all day recording. It is important to be consistent in the length of time spent recording information. Only record behaviour in the time periods set aside for the task, and make sure that the behaviour is recorded for the same length of time each day.

Data Collection

Data collection may involve simple *descriptive recording*; that is, recording briefly in writing what happened before, during and after each incident. You should have enough information to describe a reasonably consistent pattern of events that happened before and after the behaviour.

In some cases, data collection may involve counting how many times the behaviour occurs; that is, the *frequency* of occurrence. For example:

- Mark bit his hand five times today;
- Mary threw her drink twice at lunchtime;
- John hit another child four times at kindy.

At other times, data collection involves timing how long the behaviour persists each time it occurs; that is, the *duration* of the behaviour. For example:

- Billy screamed for 20 minutes after being put to bed;
- Ann cried for 5 minutes after her mother left her at preschool.

For some behaviours, it may be necessary to collect data on both the frequency and duration. For example, to reduce a child's temper tantrums, we may need to know not only how often the behaviour occurs, but how long the behaviour continues. By having both of these measures, we can see whether the tantrums are decreasing by either how often they occur or how long they continue.

Data collection will give an overall picture of the target behaviour —it allows us to notice even small changes that may not be immediately apparent without the recorded information.

The data collection must be completed before a specific program is designed and implemented. This provides a *baseline*; that is, a measure of the amount or strength of behaviour before the program is started. The baseline gives information about how often and for how long the behaviour is occurring, and provides a level of behaviour against which the results of a program can be compared. Baseline data also provide a basis for later comparison to judge the effectiveness of the management program.

Keeping a record of behaviour will:
- show whether a behaviour is increasing or decreasing;
- document even small changes in behaviour;
- indicate the severity of the target behaviour.

---

3 Recording Approaches

Recording by observation is used to record behaviour as it actually occurs. There are a number of basic approaches to recording behaviour, each with its own advantages and disadvantages. The approach selected will ultimately depend on the behaviour to be modified and the time available for recording.

Continuous or Event Recording

Event recording provides an exact count of how many times a behaviour occurs.

This is a commonly used observational recording procedure, because it directly reflects the frequency of a behaviour's occurrence. In this method, a note is made every time the child engages in the target behaviour. A count of the target behaviour is made within a specified sample observation period.

This is obviously the most appropriate method to use with target behaviours that occur infrequently; that is, behaviours that do not occur more than approximately 10 times during the observation period. When recording continuously for long periods of time (perhaps throughout the whole day), the behaviour should be recorded each and every time it happens. Event recording may only be used to measure **discrete behaviours**; that is, behaviours that have a definite beginning and end.

For example:

- the number of times that Billy hits another child;
- the number of times that Billy plays with his penis;
- the number of times that Mary bangs her head on the floor.

If a target behaviour occurs more frequently, occurs at specific times of the day or continues for longer periods of time, an accurate enough picture may be obtained by collecting data only at certain times during the day or for short periods at different times during the day.

Specific-time Recording

> Specific-time recording provides an exact account of behaviours that occur only at times during the day.

If a target behaviour occurs only in certain situations or at certain times of the day, it should be possible to collect enough accurate data during these periods to obtain a baseline.

For example:

- the number of times Billy comes out of his room at bedtime;
- the number of times Mary leaves the table at mealtimes;
- the length of time it takes Mary to stop crying after arriving at preschool;
- the length of time it takes to coax Billy into the bath at bathtime.

Specific-time recording may be completed using the same basic format as is used for event recording. However, it is important to establish whether the data collecting involves counting the frequency or the duration of the behaviour.

Interval Recording

> Interval recording does not provide an exact count of behaviours, but is appropriate for measuring continuous behaviours.

With this approach, it is possible to briefly check a child's behaviour at certain intervals during the day to determine if a particular behaviour is occurring. A specific time period is defined, during which the target behaviour is observed. This method may be used when the behaviour occurs almost continuously throughout the day. The information collected should give a reasonably accurate picture of the behaviour without having to spend the whole day collecting data. It is necessary to set aside 1 or 2 hours during the day and record the target behaviour at regular intervals, perhaps every 5 minutes, within that period.

For example:

- self-stimulatory behaviours such as rocking, hand-flapping, head-banging;
- toileting problems such as having wet pants;
- repetitive behaviours such as screaming;
- teeth-grinding.

When you decide on the best approach to use in collecting data on a particular target behaviour, it is important to remember that the reason for collecting the information is to obtain an accurate picture of the behaviour without having to spend an unreasonable amount of time observing and recording. It is therefore important to choose the approach that suits a particular schedule, but still gives an accurate picture of the child's behaviour.

Recording approaches include:

- continuous or event recording;
- specific-time recording;
- interval recording.

Consistency

An important point to remember no matter what recording method is decided upon is to ensure that there is consistency in the length of the recording periods. Target behaviours should be measured only during the time set aside for the task. If the length of the time periods is varied, then there will be marked changes in the rate of the target behaviour, which will lead to inconsistencies and inaccuracies in any inferences to be drawn from the data.

> Be consistent—always record for the same length of time each session.

4 Identifying the Behaviour Pattern

By looking beyond the problem behaviour itself to what occurs before and what follows after, it is possible to determine ways to modify the behaviour. Most problem behaviour involves give and take between the child and her surrounding environment—she uses behaviour to successfully obtain what she desires from her environment.

Example A: Billy cries when he is put to bed at night. He continues crying until his parents give in, and he is allowed to come out of his room.

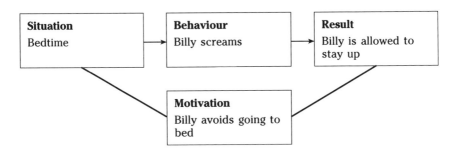

Example B: Billy screams whenever his mother takes him shopping at the supermarket. His screams are so disruptive and embarrassing that his mother gives up and goes home.

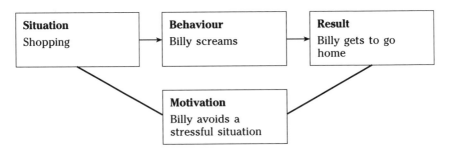

The behaviour in both examples is the same: Billy screams. At bedtime, the behaviour attracts attention from the family, along with other benefits such as staying up and watching TV. In the supermarket, the screaming makes a difficult or unwanted activity "go away".

By noting that there are different patterns to Billy's behaviour, it can be seen that there are different motivations for the same behaviour. At bedtime, Billy's family might change the consequences by ignoring Billy's tantrum and reading him a story as he quietens. Billy's mother could make the shopping expeditions less stressful by choosing a smaller grocery shop, keeping the trip short and rewarding Billy for appropriate behaviour.

By obtaining information about what happens immediately before a particular behaviour and what happens after the behaviour occurs, the child's motivation for engaging in the behaviour becomes clearer. It then becomes possible to decide on an actual behaviour-management procedure to change or modify the problem behaviour, to change and enrich aspects of the child's environment and to teach the child skills to provide alternative ways of attaining wants.

When you are recording baseline information, a record sheet that incorporates information about the situation, the target behaviour and the consequences will be most helpful when it comes to designing a program to change behaviour.

A **sample record sheet** for recording baseline information follows. The record sheet includes some essential basic information such as name, target behaviour, starting date and recording times. The information to be recorded includes:

- the **time** at which the target behaviour occurs. This information will be helpful when planning a program to change behaviour.
- the **situation** in which the target behaviour occurs. This will provide information about what is happening just before the behaviour occurs. It is important to remain objective when completing this section, as the information collected should be about what was *seen* to be happening, not what was *perceived* or *thought* to be happening.

- the **target behaviour** involves a brief description of the actual behaviour. *Be precise.* If you are recording the length of time the behaviour occurs, you may record the information here.
- the **result** of the behaviour. A brief description of what happens immediately after the behaviour should be recorded. This may include what the child says or does, what is said or done to the child, or where the child goes.

The information that is collected on the record sheet about the situation, the behaviour and the consequences will be most relevant and useful when designing a particular behaviour-management program. Baseline information should be collected for a period of at least 1 to 2 weeks. If a behaviour occurs infrequently, it may be necessary to collect data for a longer period.

Depending on the context, a problem behaviour may be dealt with in a number of different ways. Once information has been collected to indicate a pattern of behaviour; that is, an indication of the function the behaviour serves for the child, then a behaviour-management procedure can be implemented to modify the behaviour, restructure the child's environment and teach additional or alternative skills.

Graphing Baseline Information

Once baseline data have been collected, the information can be organised into an easy-to-read format. The data can be translated into graph form so that it is simple to understand at a glance what is happening. Graphs are used to obtain a clear picture of whether the target behaviour is increasing or decreasing or remaining stable.

When graphing, the vertical line generally indicates the number of times or the length of time the behaviour occurs; the vertical line is labelled according to the units of **behaviour**: for example, the number of screams or the minutes of self-stimulatory hand-flapping. The horizontal line on the graph will generally indicate the units of **time**. It could be minutes, hours, days or even weeks, depending on the target behaviour. When using the record sheet, the simplest method is to graph "days" on the horizontal axis so that a daily record of the target behaviour can be plotted.

After the vertical and horizontal axes have been marked on the graph, the information from the record sheet can be transferred to the graph, which makes it much easier to see behaviour changes.

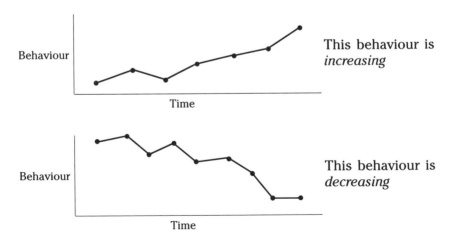

Behaviour | Time

This behaviour is *increasing*

Behaviour | Time

This behaviour is *decreasing*

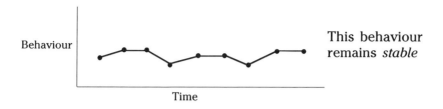

Baseline data may be easily translated into graph form. Graphs give a clear picture of whether a target behaviour is increasing or decreasing or remaining stable.

Sample

Record Sheet

Name: _____

Target behaviour: _____

_____

Recording date: _____

Time	Situation	Behaviour	Result

Sample

Record Sheet

Name: <u>Billy</u>

Target behaviour: <u>Billy screams, hits out, kicks, drops</u>
<u>to the floor, and refuses to walk</u>

Recording date: <u>July</u>

Time	Situation	Behaviour	Result
3|7 10:30	At the supermarket	Billy screamed and dropped to the floor.	Billy picked up and taken home.
5|7 1:30	On arrival at a friend's home for the party	Billy kicked mother, screamed and refused to walk.	Billy given lollies but eventually taken home.
7|7 9:30	Airport	Billy dropped to the floor and screamed.	Billy taken outside.
7|7 2:00	Shopping centre	Billy hit shop assistant-screamed and kicked mother.	Billy refused ride - taken back to car.
10|7 6:30	At restaurant	Billy refused to sit on chair, cried and yelled.	Take-away food ordered → Billy taken home.
15|7 1:00	Supermarket	Billy screamed and hit out at other shoppers.	Mother left shopping and took Billy back to car.
16|7 AM	Local shop	Billy cried, but walked with mother	Finished shopping quickly and taken outside.

PART B:
Behaviour-management Procedures

Once we are able to identify problem behaviours and begin to understand why they occur, we are ready to look at ways to manage the behaviour. There are a number of basic steps to follow if we are to successfully reduce a child's problem behaviours. We have already discussed the first three steps in some detail in Part A.

These are to:

1 *describe and specify the behaviour*—precisely, in such a way that it can be seen and measured;
2 *record and measure the behaviour*—by descriptive recording of frequency or duration to give a baseline;
3 *identify the pattern of behaviour*—look beyond the problem to what occurs before and follows after.

Once we have completed these initial steps, we are ready to undertake an appropriate management procedure to change or modify the problem behaviour. Depending on the particular behaviour and the motivation for its occurrence, we will need to look at changing the following:

- the situation in which a behaviour occurs;
- the outcome or result of the behaviour.

At the same time as we are implementing procedures to change the situation in which problem behaviour occurs or the outcome of the behaviour, it is important to:

- encourage alternative, more appropriate or socially acceptable behaviours.

The objective of any behaviour-management program is to intervene with the child so that the need for problem behaviour is reduced or eliminated. This usually involves some preventative measures, such as changing and enriching the child's environment by introducing structure and routines, teaching the child to choose, and expanding his interests and activities. It also involves teaching the child skills to be able to obtain what he wants by alternative means.

It is also necessary to have an immediate response ready for when the behaviour does occur, so that the child becomes aware that it is no longer an effective means of achieving what he wants.

Finally, it is also necessary to respond positively to the child for appropriate behaviour—to encourage alternative, more socially acceptable behaviours.

Continue to Measure Behaviour

In addition to collecting data on a child's behaviour before initiating a program, it is essential to continue to keep records after a management program is initiated. These records will be useful in determining whether a particular program is successful.

Data collection should be kept up throughout the behaviour-management program to ensure that the program is successfully decreasing the problem behaviour. It is important to continue to record the behaviour the same way that data was collected during the baseline period.

After collecting data for a set period of time (either days or weeks, depending on the specific problem behaviour), it will be obvious whether the behaviour-management strategy is working. If the behaviour is not decreasing, it will be necessary to look closely at the program:

1 Have you overlooked a medical problem that may be contributing to the behaviour problem?
2 Have you correctly identified the outcome that is motivating the problem?
3 Have you inadvertently changed the outcome?
4 Are other carers and family members also consistently carrying out the program?
5 Are you encouraging alternative behaviour?
6 Have you arranged the situation so that the behaviour is less likely to occur again?
7 Have you taught the child some necessary skills to allow him alternative ways of attaining what he wants?
8 Have you restructured the child's environment so that the need for problem behaviour is reduced?

Chapter 6
Changing the Situation

By studying the situation in which problem behaviours occur (that is, by observing what happened just before the problem behaviour), it may be possible to prevent the recurrence of a particular behaviour simply by modifying the situation.

In certain situations, a child may be encouraged to behave in a particular way. For example, when a child is tired or hungry, he may become more demanding and uncooperative; when a child is placed in an unfamiliar or overwhelming situation, he may become anxious, withdrawn or aggressive; or when a child does not understand what is expected of him, he may become frustrated or angry. Behaviour is a means of communication, and the child is communicating his distress, frustration or anger. There are certain times, places and events where problem behaviours are more likely to occur.

Modifying the Situation

Warn the Child about Possible Changes in the Normal Routine

Some children do not usually cope well with changes in their normal routines. Unexpected changes can lead to frustration and tantrums. Wherever possible, a sense of structure and routine should be maintained both at home and at preschool to help the child cope. However, every child must learn to cope occasionally in unexpected and unpredictable situations, which will occur throughout life. One common cause of frustration among young children occurs when the child does not understand what is happening around him. It is important, therefore, to ensure that explanations and information are given to the child in a way that he can understand so that he has at least some understanding of what to expect in the unfamiliar situation.

Discuss a change of plans with the child, let him know where you are going, how long you will be and always reinforce the fact that you will be returning home (or to other familiar situations). Remember to keep language simple and to the point in any discussions or explanation. Many children have auditory comprehension problems and may find it difficult to follow lengthy explanations. As some children have superior visual skills, it may be a good idea to incorporate a visual presentation of relevant information using photos, line drawings and gestures.

Parents should be aware that many misunderstandings occur around everyday events that they assume are familiar to the child. Even minor changes to a familiar routine still may be quite stressful to a child. Be more careful and offer information and explanations in unfamiliar situations.

Provide Something Familiar in an Unfamiliar Situation

It may be a favourite toy or an activity that will allow the child to associate something positive and enjoyable with the new situation (for example, buy an ice cream or let the child have a coin-operated ride in a new shopping centre).

Model Appropriate Behaviour

One method of demonstrating appropriate behaviour to a child is to role model the behaviour, or to reward *other* children in his presence for demonstrating appropriate behaviour. This method usually works as a two-part strategy of ignoring problem behaviour and encouraging appropriate behaviour by reward; that is, ignore the child during problem behaviour and at the same time, praise *someone else* for appropriate behaviour.

For example:

- When Billy refuses to pick up his toys, ignore him and say, "Good girl, Mary, for picking up *your* toys."
- When Mary is running around the room at lunchtime, ignore her and say, "You are sitting up beautifully at the table, James, and eating your sandwich."

Teach Alternative Methods of Communicating and Behaving

It is important to teach skills to young children when you are developing behaviour-management strategies. In addition to encouraging alternative behaviours that are incompatible with the problem behaviour, it is important to teach the child a number of new skills and behaviours.

For example:

- If Billy continually throws his toys, he may need to learn some different and more appropriate ways to play with his toys.
- If Mary screams and hits out when she wants something, teach her to point to pictures to communicate her needs.

If a child has a variety of behaviours to choose from in a particular situation, he may be less likely to choose a problem behaviour.

Ensure that Activities Are Age Appropriate and Enjoyable

During a teaching session and during routine activities at home, it is essential to look closely at the content of any activity in which the child is involved to ensure that it is within his present abilities and is not too difficult. Activities should always be enjoyable and motivating for the child—problem behaviour often occurs when a child is attempting to avoid an unpleasant or difficult activity or task.

Give Physical or Verbal Assistance

Often, a child may not understand other people's expectations in certain situations. Occasional physical or verbal prompts may be all that are required to show the child how to behave appropriately.
For example:

- Billy is given some physical assistance to retrieve his ball whenever it rolls out of reach.
- Mary is given a verbal prompt to wait until it is her turn to play with the toy, which should be phrased in a positive way as "Good waiting."

Ensure the Environment Is "Child Proof"

Instead of constantly reminding the child not to touch certain objects for fear of breakage or damage, perhaps it is time to develop some lateral thinking. You cannot always remove the child from the situation, but perhaps you can remove the treasured objects until such time as the child responds appropriately to a firm, "No! Don't touch."

Rather than keep Billy in the playpen to preserve the Christmas tree, Billy's mother thought of an alternative that kept everyone happy and involved a little lateral thinking.

Billy's mother put the Christmas tree in the playpen and left Billy the freedom to play unrestricted. This solution may be tried with different objects—the TV, video player, record player, etc.

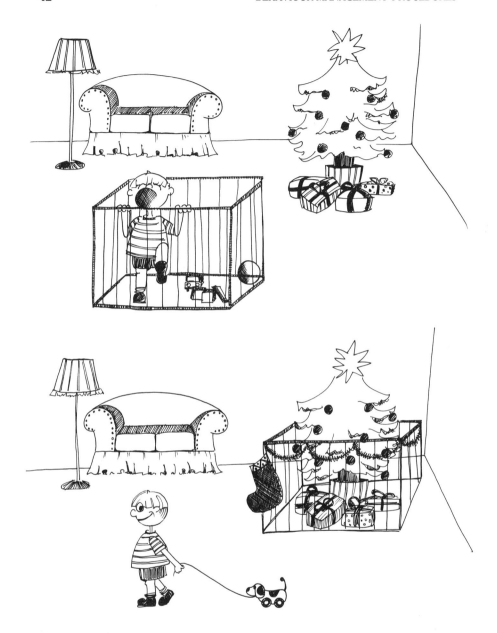

Reward Appropriate Behaviour in Different Situations

It is essential to continually reinforce a child's appropriate behaviour. Some children do not generalise behaviour across different situations, and need to be constantly praised whenever they are doing the right thing. By continually encouraging children to behave appropriately in a number of different situations, they may eventually learn to generalise these positive behaviours to all situations. Probably the most common mistake that parents make with their child is to ignore appropriate behaviour and reward the child's problem behaviour. Parents may not think to attend to their child when everything is going well, but do pay attention (often by scolding, yelling or smacking) when the child is misbehaving.

For example, while shopping at the supermarket, you are in a hurry, and Billy is behaving appropriately. He sits quietly in the shopping trolley while you do the shopping and pay little attention to him.

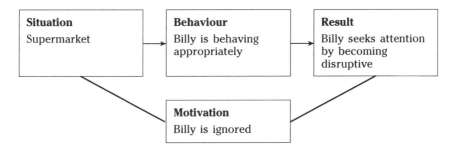

But while shopping, Billy becomes bored and begins to whine and demand to get down from the shopping trolley. You immediately chastise him, tell him to be quiet and eventually leave with the shopping not done.

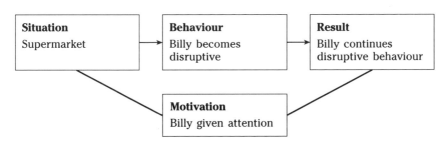

If you look closely at the example, you can see that Billy's good behaviour was ignored while his problem behaviour was rewarded with attention. This means that Billy's problem behaviour will be more likely to occur next time you are in the supermarket.

It is important to remember that some children do not differentiate between positive and negative attention. Even scolding and smacking may be rewarding to some children who will seek any kind of attention from their parents—even a spanking.

> Catch your child being good and reward appropriate behaviour.

Keep Instructions Simple and Realistic

Occasionally, problem behaviours occur despite the fact that you are teaching new skills and showing the child what is appropriate. When this occurs, ignoring the child or taking the child out of the situation are not effective, because the child is not seeking attention but rather may be trying to avoid an unpleasant task. In this case, it is essential to look closely to ensure that your expectations are within the child's present capabilities and are not too difficult.

An important part of any play session is to set the stage for success—to arrange the situation in such a way that the child finds activities within his capabilities so that he can readily succeed. This involves gearing demands to the child's level of functioning, and increasing them gradually by small steps; choosing easy-to-manage materials; giving understandable directions and eliminating distractions.

For example:

- Arranging the situation: Billy's mother organised a short play session and kept her demands very simple. She continued to encourage Billy despite any tantrum behaviour.
- Encouraging alternative behaviour: Billy's mother rewarded him immediately for sitting quietly and paying attention.

There are countless times during the day when changing a situation reduces the likelihood of problem behaviour, by simply distracting the child away from a difficult situation, or redirecting the child, removing breakable objects, providing an alternative toy or giving the child something enjoyable to do.

Although it is often necessary to change the situation in order to reduce the problem behaviour, you should also remember that it is not in the family's best interests to continually accommodate the child to such an extent that the rest of the family suffers. The child must gradually learn to adapt to the world around him. This is best done by enriching the child's environment and providing the child with additional skills to allow him to cope in different situations.

Chapter 7
Changing the Outcome or Result

In order to change the problem behaviours in young children that are causing concern, it is necessary to look carefully at the outcomes that have been maintaining the behaviours. Children usually behave according to expected outcomes, to do things that are rewarding and to avoid things that are unpleasant or non-rewarding.

Before we can hope to reduce problem behaviour, it is important to determine and understand the factors that are involved in maintaining and reinforcing these behaviours. Behaviours that are followed by a positive outcome are more likely to continue. Behaviours that are not followed by a pleasant outcome are more likely to decrease. Once we are able to understand behaviours in terms of the outcomes for the child, it becomes easier to plan strategies for change. To modify a certain behaviour, it may be necessary to alter the consequence that has been rewarding the child and motivating the behaviour.

How Do We Modify the Consequences of Problem Behaviours?

In order to modify problem behaviour, it is often necessary to change the consequences that have been maintaining it. This may involve ensuring either that no rewards are given for problem behaviours, rewards are given for appropriate behaviour, or that an unpleasant consequence follows problem behaviours. Preferably, focus on the positive or non-reinforcement outcome, rather than the use of aversive outcome.

A reinforcer is any object or event that maintains or increases the future occurrence of the behaviour it follows. Reinforcement is the procedure by which a reinforcer is delivered following a behaviour, thus strengthening that behaviour.

The use of positive reinforcement for appropriate behaviour or the lack of any reinforcement for problem behaviour are the most common management procedures to use with young children.

Often, a much more effective method, and a simpler one, is to re-direct the child to a more appropriate activity.

Ignore the Behaviour

Ignoring means that we do not respond in any way to the problem behaviour—either positively by giving into the child's demands, or negatively by scolding or smacking. In this way, the child may eventually learn that there is no reward for problem behaviour.

Ignoring is one of the most effective methods of reducing problem behaviours. However, it is also one of the most difficult methods to implement consistently and successfully over a long period of time. If you ignore behaviour as a management technique, ensure that there is nothing the child can do to force you to pay attention to her problem behaviour. It is not easy for parents to totally ignore problem behaviours, especially if the behaviours are disruptive; parents need to be reminded that they are actually ignoring the problem behaviours and not ignoring the child.

Most children enjoy and look for attention. When a child is ignored for certain behaviours, she soon begins to understand when attention is not forthcoming. If certain behaviours are consistently ignored, she soon learns to understand what causes this lack of attention and, at the same time, she determines what behaviours lead to positive attention. If the child desires a pleasant outcome such as attention, she eventually learns to behave more appropriately.

In order to decide on a proper and successful course of action when ignoring a specific problem behaviour, it is important to clearly define the actual behaviour to be ignored.

For example, Billy screams and drops to the floor whenever he is refused something he wants.

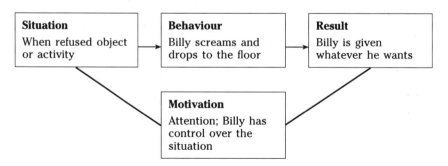

If the attention is not given and the parents are able to ignore the behaviour consistently, then eventually Billy will realise that the problem behaviour does not produce the preferred result.

At such times, the most effective way to ignore behaviours such as screaming or tantrums is to leave the situation, withdraw to another room and, if necessary, turn on the TV or read a book to distract you from the problem behaviour. This ensures that attention is not inadvertently given to the child.

It is important to remember that the behaviour may get worse before it improves. Remain consistent and don't give up.

For example, Billy climbs all over his mother, pulling her hair and interrupting conversations whenever she is talking on the telephone.

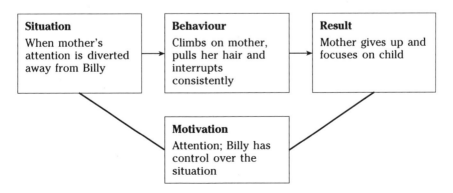

Situation	**Behaviour**	**Result**
When mother's attention is diverted away from Billy	Climbs on mother, pulls her hair and interrupts consistently	Mother gives up and focuses on child

Motivation
Attention; Billy has control over the situation

In this case, a slightly different approach may be more effective. It is difficult to leave this situation, yet Billy must learn that he cannot manipulate people or events for his own benefit. Billy's mother should continue her conversation, remove him from her lap, look away, say nothing to him and give him no attention.

The most effective method for ignoring problem behaviours depends on the actual behaviour and also on what management strategies parents are most comfortable with. Parents will eventually develop their own preferred strategies: the important fact to remember is that the child's behaviour is being ignored so as not to reward the child with attention.

Note: **For most children, the response to ignoring problem behaviour is quite predictable. Initially, the child will try even harder to gain attention. These behaviours have always worked previously and the conclusion she comes to is that she must try even harder to obtain the usual reaction. In all probability, therefore, the child's behaviour will become worse before improving. She needs to test the new reaction she is getting to her behaviour before she begins to accept it. It is during this period that parents should be aware of what is happening and why. Parents must remain firm and consistent in their approach and continue to ignore the behaviour even when it appears to be worsening.**

If the child responds positively by ceasing the behaviour, always try to find an appropriate behaviour to praise. It is essential to offer lots of attention for appropriate behaviour, whenever it occurs, especially after ignoring problem behaviour.

Hints for Ignoring Behaviour

- Ignoring means just that—doing nothing and giving no attention to the child either in a positive or a negative way, that is, no smacking, yelling, muttering, coaxing or chastising in any way.
- Ignoring may involve sitting or standing perfectly still, not looking at the child and remaining expressionless.
- Ignoring may involve leaving the room to avoid giving any reaction.
- Ignoring may involve paying attention to someone else and praising him or her for appropriate behaviour.
- Ignoring may mean avoiding the child by watching TV or reading a book.
- Giving attention to the child in a positive way when the problem behaviour decreases or stops or immediately she starts behaving appropriately.

CAUTION

Before ignoring behaviours that could be caused by something other than attention-seeking behaviour—for example, medical or physical reasons such as earache or stomachache—parents should not ignore the behaviour, but look carefully at the pattern of behaviour to determine whether some other motivation is causing the behaviour. These other possibilities should be checked thoroughly before commencing any program of ignoring problem behaviour.

Remove the Rewards

In certain situations, as well as ignoring the child, it may be necessary to remove tangible rewards as well. Sometimes, it is easier and more effective to take away something tangible.

For example:

- Take away Billy's food for 1 minute whenever he gets up from the table during mealtimes.
- Take the toy away from Billy for 5 minutes after he throws it.

- Remove the book from Mary for 2 minutes when she tears the pages.
- Turn off the television until Mary stops screaming.

Whenever this procedure is implemented, it is important to ensure that the child is able to retrieve whatever has been removed. The simplest method is to remove the reward for a certain period of time (usually short—for example, 2–5 minutes) or until certain behaviours have decreased or stopped. When removing the reward, if possible, the child should be told simply and directly why it is being removed. For example, "Billy, I am taking the toy away because you threw it." Focus on a behavioural statement to avoid making judgements.

As soon as the time limit is up and the behaviour has decreased, the child should be given the opportunity to have the reward returned and given praise for behaving appropriately.

Reward Appropriate Behaviour

Some problem behaviours are particularly difficult to ignore. Behaviours such as head-banging, hand-biting, hitting or throwing may require additional strategies, such as offering the child a reward for not engaging in the particular behaviour. In this situation, the reward is paired with an appropriate behaviour rather than the reward being removed for problem behaviour. Eventually, the child may be encouraged and motivated to behave appropriately and the problem behaviour should decrease.

For example, at home, Billy would often put objects up his nose or in his ears.

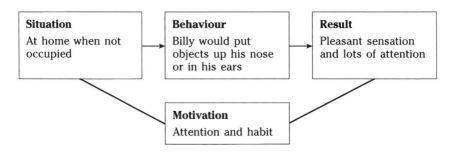

This behaviour is quite difficult to ignore as it is likely that Billy has already done substantial damage to both his nasal passages and eardrums. The behaviour does not occur at preschool, so it can be assumed that it occurs when Billy is not stimulated and that it has become a habit at home.

In this situation, a two-part strategy may be employed.

Undesirable Behaviours: Remove Rewards

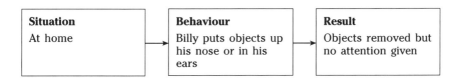

Situation	Behaviour	Result
At home	Billy puts objects up his nose or in his ears	Objects removed but no attention given

Desirable Behaviours: Give Rewards

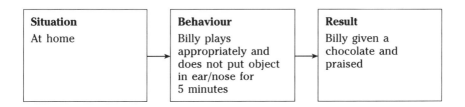

Situation	Behaviour	Result
At home	Billy plays appropriately and does not put object in ear/nose for 5 minutes	Billy given a chocolate and praised

In this situation, it is not possible to ignore the behaviour completely or to remove a tangible reward. It is, however, possible to give minimal attention to the behaviour and to offer a tangible reward for not engaging in the problem behaviour. The reward offered must be substantial enough to be more reinforcing to Billy than the motivation for the problem behaviour. Billy should also be offered the reward at regular intervals and the reward must be immediate (for example, when a timer sounds every 5 minutes). The intervals between rewards may gradually be extended over time as the problem behaviour decreases.

Rewarding appropriate behaviours and ignoring the problem behaviour are two of the most successful methods of decreasing problem behaviour. This combination has many advantages over the typical approach of punishing the child to modify behaviour. Rewards teach the child appropriate behaviour; punishment may only teach the child to avoid you, or to do something that causes trouble.

Redirect the Child

Often, the most effective method of reducing or eliminating a problem behaviour is simply to redirect the child to something else— either another activity or another part of the house. This is especially effective with young children and is much less stressful to the child and to parents.

Redirection is most effective if it is carried out before the problem behaviour is established. As soon as a child begins to become agitated or is in a situation where she is unlikely to cope, she should be redirected or given some assistance. Redirection may be physical—that is, actually removing the child from a particular situation; it may be verbal, as in modifying instructions or directions; or situational—for example, changing or modifying an activity or task that the child is finding too difficult.

When ignoring problem behaviour, expect it to get worse before it gets better.

Use rewards to increase appropriate behaviour and, whenever possible, ignore inappropriate behaviour.

Reward consistently and immediately after appropriate behaviour occurs.

Redirect the child to a more appropriate activity or situation if she appears not to be coping.

Punish the Problem Behaviour

Punishment is a procedure that in theory decreases the future probability of a behaviour. Research, however, does not support the theory.

Three punishment techniques that have been used in behaviour management are:

1 *Response cost*—implies that an inappropriate response "costs" something of value such as earned rewards or privileges.
2 *Time out*—for a specified brief period of time, the child is isolated from social interaction that may reinforce the problem behaviour.
3 *Overcorrection*—implies requiring the child to make restitution for damages, or positive practice in which the child is required to practice repeatedly a more correct form of behaviour for a short period. There is little evidence available that overcorrection is at all effective.

Without question, positive reinforcement for appropriate behaviour is of primary importance in behaviour-management strategies. Occasionally, we come across problem behaviours that do not respond to any of these strategies and seem to require punishment. Extreme care is necessary in the use of any physical punishment.

Punishment should only be used in circumstances of extreme danger, such as for behaviours that cause injury to self or others.

In order to be a humane and effective control technique, punishment should be:

1 used only when positive methods fail and when the continuance of the behaviour will result in more stress than the punishment itself;

2 administered only by people who are warm and loving in their relationships with the child and who are able to offer positive reinforcement for appropriate behaviour;

3 administered calmly and matter-of-factly, following a carefully defined procedure in order to avoid an emotional reaction, such as anger or threats;

4 administered fairly consistently and immediately after the behaviour has occurred;

5 reasonable in severity and wherever possible related to the problem behaviour itself (for example, helping to repair a broken object).

6 Punishment should, whenever possible, involve a loss of rewards. A loss of privileges is preferable to other forms of punishment.

7 Spanking should never be used as a form of punishment.

Punishment techniques in behaviour management include response cost, time out and overcorrection.

Response Cost

Response cost involves the withdrawal of a specified amount of reinforcers dependent upon an expected response from the child. The removal of rewards such as tokens, lollies, use of a toy or time watching television, contingent upon a certain response, are illustrations of response cost. For example, Mary enjoys watching *Sesame Street* on television in the afternoon. She is denied access to the program if she refuses to help pack away her toys.

Technically, response cost differs from physical punishment in that punishment involves the presentation of an aversive stimulus, such as a smack, rather than the withdrawal of a certain amount of reinforcers to reduce the occurrence of a problem behaviour. Removing a child's dessert because she misbehaves during dinner is a response-cost procedure. Smacking the child for the behaviour is punishment if it reduces the rate of the behaviour.

The response-cost procedure is usually limited to the withdrawal of exchangeable or other conditioned reinforcers like grades, points or tokens. It can be a convenient system, especially when used in conjunction with a token system or loss of privileges. As soon as an unwanted behaviour occurs, a token is removed immediately, quietly and with little physical effort. Because response cost can be used so conveniently, it is probably used more often than it should. Used with discretion, and only with more able children, it can prove an efficient technique for eliminating a particular problem behaviour with minimal disruption to other activities.

Time Out

Time out is a form of punishment that requires a period of time without any reinforcement. It should be structured so that rewards of any kind are denied to the child for a specified period of time. Time out involves placing a child in a situation where any possibility of reward is removed entirely for a specified period of time, usually between 2 and 5 minutes. It may be used to diffuse a difficult situation where no immediate alternative management procedure is available and both child and adults are extremely stressed.

When a behaviour is so disruptive that ignoring it is difficult or ineffective and there are no tangible rewards to remove, it may be necessary to implement a more intensive time out strategy.

Certain guidelines should be carefully followed when using a time out strategy for problem behaviours. This will allow the child to understand exactly what is happening and why.

- Explain in advance what problem behaviours will result in time out. Tell the child what will happen should the specified behaviour occur.

- Decide or a location for time out. This may involve sitting the child on the floor or a chair away from other people, placing the child in her room for a short period of time, or sending the child outside into an enclosed area. Ensure that the time out area provides no opportunities for further problem behaviour or stimulation.

- Specify the length of time out period beforehand. This should be kept short to avoid distress to the child or parents.

- When problem behaviour occurs, tell the child to go to time out and physically assist if necessary. Ignore any attempts by the child to avoid going to time out. Do not look at or speak to the child apart from giving the simple command: "No hitting! Go time out."

- When the child is in time out, ignore any further inappropriate behaviours such as screaming, kicking, throwing objects. If the child attempts to stand up and leave time out prematurely, immediately return her to the time out area, giving minimal attention.

- Set a timer to measure length of time out (2–5 minutes). The child must remain in time out until the timer rings.

- The child's exit from time out should be completed with minimal attention. However, you should find appropriate behaviours to reward with praise and attention when the child returns to the previous situation. This is the time to emphasise the types of behaviour that will always lead to approval and attention.

Overcorrection

Overcorrection is a procedure that was developed by Foxx and Azrin (1972) to reduce problem behaviour. It is a specific type of mild punishment designed to minimise the negative reactions caused by intense punishment. It has two basic components: to overcorrect the environmental effects of an inappropriate action, and to require the child to intensely practise overcorrect forms of appropriate relevant behaviour.

Overcorrection means either:

- requiring the child to make restitution for damages (perhaps helping to repair broken objects; or picking up all the toys thrown and all other toys in the room);

- positive practice, in which the child is required to practice a more correct form of behaviour repeatedly for a short time. For example, posting objects into a post box rather than putting them up the nose or in the ear; or carefully turning the pages of a book rather than repeatedly tearing them.

Like punishment, overcorrection is an aversive procedure, and most of the time, disadvantages exist as for punishment, though generally to a lesser extent because of the milder nature of overcorrection. It should be used with caution and never in isolation, and its potential side effects should be constantly monitored. Under optimal conditions, the educational value of overcorrection may overshadow the aversive aspect, and help to develop new and more appropriate behaviours. However, it is intrusive and aversive, and the repeated acts of restitution and positive practice can interfere with the child's participation in other, more appropriate activities. In general, the child is not provided with alternative, more functional and acceptable ways to behave. Overcorrection is therefore best reserved for extremely resistant behaviours, those that are seriously disruptive or dangerous, or situations in which few, more appropriate, alternative behaviours are available to be encouraged.

Occasionally, the above strategies may not appear to be working, especially with some very serious, ingrained problem behaviours. These are often harmful to the child and cause extreme anxiety and stress to families. If the above strategies have been tried consistently and are not effective, then it may be necessary to look at the use of physical punishment (aversives). The use of aversives should only ever be considered in extreme cases and should only ever be implemented and monitored by qualified professionals.

The Use of Aversives: Physical Punishment

The use of aversives means that the problem behaviour is followed by an unpleasant or disliked experience. Examples of physical punishment include smacking, shaking, pulling hair or biting back when bitten. Evidence suggests that the use of aversives does not work— the effect only seems to last in the presence of the punisher, so it is not a lasting method of modifying problem behaviour.

Many parents have found that a well-timed spanking will occasionally work to eliminate annoying and potentially dangerous problem behaviours. However, it is important to realise that when you hit or spank a child, you are demonstrating a form of behaviour that she may imitate. A young child, especially, does not understand the maxim, "Do as I say, not as I do." You may, therefore, end up with a child who becomes more aggressive and develops worse behaviours. When physically punishing a child, you are giving her attention, even though it is negative. The child may look on this as a form of attention, which then motivates rather than decreases the problem behaviour.

The use of physical punishment is a controversial one and it involves some major moral and ethical issues. Relative to the other strategies discussed above, a child is taught very little through physical punishment and it is certainly unpleasant for any family member to implement it systematically and consistently. It is therefore better to avoid the use of physical punishment and think of an alternative strategy.

> Before using any of the above punishment techniques, you should try to reduce a target behaviour by ignoring it, redirecting the child and rewarding appropriate behaviour. Physical punishment is not recommended as an effective procedure for reducing problem behaviour. Consistency, immediate response and rewarding appropriate behaviour are the keys to the most effective use of punishment. Always tell the child simply exactly why the punishment is occurring.

Chapter 8
Encouraging Alternative Behaviours

As well as implementing a behaviour-management strategy to change or modify problem behaviours, a child should be encouraged to learn some alternative, more appropriate ways to behave.

Certain behaviours may not seem to be inappropriate to a small child. If a particular behaviour has previously achieved its objective, the child will continue to engage in the behaviour until such time as the consequences change. If the child is no longer rewarded or no longer manages to avoid a situation, he is likely to seek alternative methods to achieve his objective. It is therefore important to offer the child a more socially acceptable way of achieving his objective, and to reinforce the behaviour when it occurs. Alternative appropriate behaviours should always be followed by pleasant, rewarding consequences.

Appropriate alternative behaviours to be rewarded are usually quite easy to determine because they are always incompatible with the problem behaviour; that is, they cannot occur at the same time as the problem behaviour. Therefore, when motivating the child to behave appropriately, reward behaviours that are incompatible with the problem behaviour.

For example, Billy would continually whine, cry or have tantrums whenever he wanted anything.

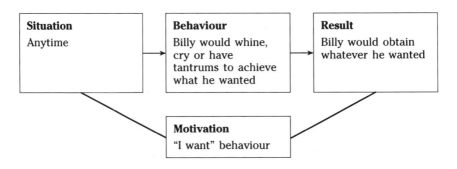

Situation	Behaviour	Result
Anytime	Billy would whine, cry or have tantrums to achieve what he wanted	Billy would obtain whatever he wanted

Motivation
"I want" behaviour

There was nothing wrong with the fact that Billy wanted to have certain things. The problem lay in the way that Billy set about achieving his objective and his response to his wishes being denied.

Billy's family set about finding an alternative, appropriate way for Billy to achieve his objective that was incompatible with the whining, crying behaviour. The appropriate behaviour was then rewarded or reinforced, and the incompatible, problem behaviour was ignored and discouraged. He was rewarded only when he behaved appropriately. This may have involved teaching Billy new skills such as pointing, signing, or verbal communication as well as structuring his environment to make it easy for him to choose what he wanted.

> For undesirable behaviours, remove the rewards.
> For desirable behaviours, give the rewards.

Undesirable Behaviour: Remove Rewards

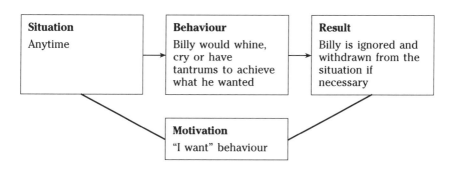

Desirable Behaviour: Give Rewards

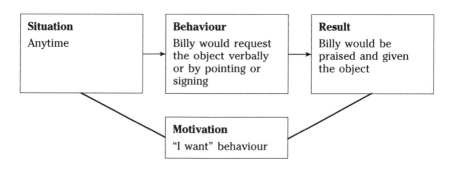

Once Billy has learned that he is more likely to achieve his objective (to obtain what he wants) by behaving appropriately, then the screaming, whining behaviours should decrease. Billy has also learned some new skills and his environment has been enriched, so that he may eventually generalise these skills to other situations, and there should be an improvement in his general behaviour as his frustration levels decrease.

Billy will eventually need to learn that there are times when it is not possible to achieve his objective, no matter how appropriately he asks. It is important to manage such situations by:

- being fair and granting reasonable requests. However, if you say No, then remain firm and do not give in because of problem behaviour. It is important to remain consistent and firm so that the child will eventually learn to accept when you say No. Be sure to praise the child for calmly accepting the denial of a request.

- avoiding situations where the temptations are just too great; for example, the lolly aisle at the supermarket, or the toy store.

- setting the ground rules at the start. If you are going to the shopping centre, let the child know before you arrive at the store that he cannot have a ride today.

- being ready to divert the child's attention, to distract him away from certain activities or objects by having him help you. For example, "Can you carry this bag for me."

Another example: Mary refuses to remain in her bedroom at bedtime. She continually gets out of bed and leaves her room requesting drinks, cuddles, more TV or says she is scared. When she is put back to bed, she cries and screams.

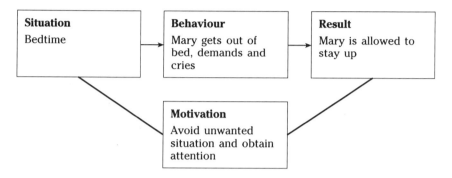

Undesirable Behaviour: Remove Rewards

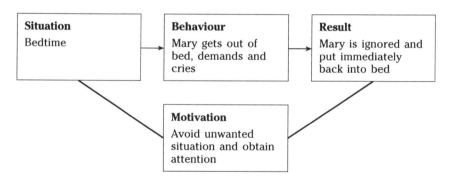

Desirable Behaviour: Give Rewards

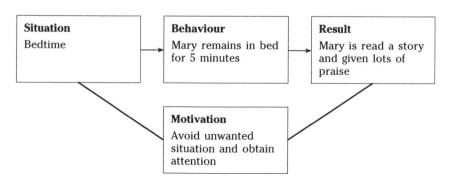

When Mary remains in bed for a short period of time, she is given lots of attention and the situation is made more rewarding by reading her a story. As Mary learns to behave more appropriately and remain in bed, her parents may gradually lengthen the time before she is read a story until she remains quite happily in bed without the need for tangible reinforcements. In this way, Mary learns a new routine and her bedtime is a positive and rewarding experience, making the need to object and avoid the situation unnecessary.

Additional Techniques

Occasionally, a behaviour that you wish to increase does not occur so that you cannot reward it. For example, if the child never packs his toys away, how can you get this behaviour to occur regularly? There are several ways to teach a child new behaviours and skills.

Telling

It may be necessary to remind the child how to respond in an appropriate way in a given situation. The child may know the correct response, but not do it without being told. When you are telling the child to do something, be concise and to the point. For example, if you are leaving and saying goodbye to the child, you may need to remind the child to say goodbye. Reward the child immediately for a correct response.

Modelling

The child may learn by imitating the behaviours of others, especially parents, siblings and peers. You may need to model appropriate behaviour and show the child what is expected in a given situation. For example, if you want the child to feed himself with a spoon, you should tell the child, "Pick up the spoon." If the child does not follow the command, you should repeat the request and also give a physical prompt by pointing to the spoon, or model the correct response by picking up the spoon yourself. Repeat the request, and if he does pick up the spoon, then reward the child immediately. If he does not, you may have to actually guide the child's hand to pick it up.

Physical Prompts

The child may need to be physically guided to learn a new behaviour. Always use the least amount of guidance necessary to help the child learn a new behaviour. Encourage the child to do as much of the activity as possible and only assist when necessary.

Fading

Fading is simply the gradual reduction of any physical assistance. When fading assistance, do it gradually and continue to reward improvements in behaviour as they occur. This technique is usually most successful in teaching new tasks, because the child always achieves success and is rewarded for it.

Shaping

Sometimes behaviour can be shaped to an appropriate response. When shaping, you work towards an appropriate behaviour by starting to reward behaviour that may only vaguely resemble the final behaviour. Shaping may be used when teaching quite complicated skills such as dressing, feeding and socialising with others. For example, when teaching a child to dress himself, you would need to reward gradual, small improvements in the skill over a period of time until the child was able to complete the task independently.

An important part of any behaviour-management program is to encourage the child to behave appropriately. This may be achieved by modifying the child's environment, rewarding the child for behaving in an acceptable way and by teaching the child skills to help him to cope and reduce frustration.

Telling, modelling and physically prompting are techniques for assisting the child perform an appropriate behaviour. Fading is simply the gradual reduction of any assistance. Shaping is the technique of rewarding closer and closer approximations to the appropriate behaviour.

Summary

The general approach to behaviour management may be summarised in a few simple steps.

1 Identify and *specify exactly* the problem behaviour. Is it enough of a problem to warrant a program to change it?

2   *Observe* the behaviour and look at what happens before and after it occurs. Try to identify the *motivation* for the behaviour.

3   *Measure* the behaviour to see how often it occurs and how long it lasts (baseline).

4   Find a *pattern* in the behaviour.

5   Plan and implement a systematic approach to change the behaviour involving:

    a   changing what usually happens *before* the behaviour;

    b   changing the *consequences* of the behaviour;

    c   encouraging *alternative* appropriate behaviour and teaching additional skills.

6   *Continue measuring* the behaviour to ensure that the approach is working—if it isn't working, make changes in the approach or try something new.

7   Ensure that there are positive consequences available to *encourage* the new behaviour.

PART C:
Strategies for Managing Specific Problem Behaviours

In this section, a number of examples of common problem behaviours and some strategies for dealing with them are discussed. Although strategies are listed to help parents and carers deal with specific problem behaviours, this section should not be used in isolation. It is important to understand and collect information on when, where, how and, most importantly, why problem behaviours occur before implementing any particular management procedures. It is recommended that you read Parts A and B before undertaking any specific strategies—you need to look beyond the behaviour itself to what occurs before, what happens after and the functional message in the behaviour.

These strategies are merely suggestions to put you on the right track. Often, it is a matter of trial and error—remember that every child is different and what works with one child may not work with another. Some of these strategies may be useful for a particular situation, others will be inappropriate.

The basic model for managing problem behaviours involves a number of steps that should be followed systematically. The first step is to determine why the child is behaving in a particular way—what is the message the child is trying to convey? It is necessary to look at the function of the behaviour in a particular context to answer this question.

The second step in any behaviour-management program is to find ways to decrease or increase a particular behaviour by restructuring the child's environment, teaching the child new skills, responding to the behaviour when it occurs in such a way that the child learns that the behaviour is no longer effective and encouraging alternative, more appropriate behaviour from the child.

Rewards

Rewards are used extensively in any behaviour-management program. The aim is to show the child, by rewarding her, what behaviours are appropriate for a given situation.

When using rewards to motivate children, it is important to remember:

- rewards are individual reinforcers—what works for one child may not work for another;
- rewards are only classed as reinforcers if they are actually responsible for changes in behaviour;
- praise is a non-tangible reward—it works for some children and not for others;
- lollies, chips, visits to favourite fast-food outlets are tangible rewards—they also do not always work for all children;
- most programs involving rewards tend to try to progress to the point where the child is responding to non-tangible rewards rather than tangible rewards;
- before using rewards to encourage appropriate behaviour, it is necessary to determine what reinforces the child to behave in a certain way—this will allow you to choose possible rewards that are motivating for the child.

> The aim of any behaviour-management program is always to decrease problem behaviours and at the same time, to encourage the child to develop alternative, more appropriate ways to behave.

Chapter 9

Managing Problem Behaviours at Home

- Aggression against Others
- Bathtime
- Bedtime Tantrums
- Compulsive Behaviours: Opening and Closing Doors
- Eating Problems
- Fussy Eaters

- Gaze Avoidance
- Masturbation
- Obsessive Behaviours and Obsession with Objects
- Screaming
- Self-abuse
- Shopping
- Sleeping in Parents' Bed

- Spinning Objects
- Stripping Clothing
- Teeth-cleaning
- Throwing Objects
- Toe-walking
- Toileting
- Travelling by Car

Aggression against Others

This problem behaviour cannot be ignored. However, minimal attention should be given during any management program that is implemented *immediately* the act of aggression occurs. The child

67

should also be taught more socially acceptable ways to behave as an alternative to the aggressive behaviour. Aggression is an example of the child's use of behaviour as an alternative to language—often the child acts through frustration. It is therefore important to encourage different means of communication in order to decrease the child's frustration levels. Some children do not know how to interact appropriately and they have a poorly developed awareness of the consequences of their actions on others. Other times, the aggression may be a form of attention-seeking behaviour.

Intervention Strategies

- Define the behaviour exactly.
- Act *immediately* the act of aggression occurs, not later.
- Remove the child from the situation giving minimal attention—have her sit on the floor (or chair or beanbag).
- Say, "No hitting" (biting/kicking/pinching, etc.) firmly—give no other verbal comments.
- Give the child no eye contact.
- Once the child is sitting, immediately give attention to the child who is hurt.
- After 2–5 minutes, return the child to the previous situation with no further comment.
- Make sure that the child is returned to the previous situation and not allowed to move immediately on to a new activity—this is to ensure that the child does not use aggression as a means of avoiding an unwanted situation.
- Check the situation closely to see if it is necessary to make some changes to prevent the behaviour occurring again.
- Model appropriate interaction—it is essential to give the child an alternative way to behave.

For example, at preschool when Billy is expected to share toys, he becomes upset and will hit or bite the other children.

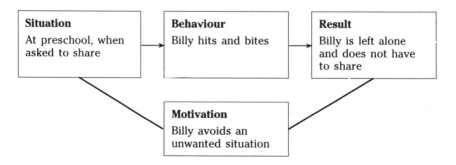

Situation	Behaviour	Result
At preschool, when asked to share	Billy hits and bites	Billy is left alone and does not have to share

Motivation
Billy avoids an unwanted situation

Two-part Management Strategy

Undesirable Behaviour: Ignore

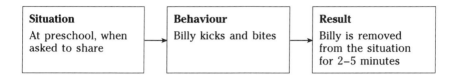

Situation	Behaviour	Result
At preschool, when asked to share	Billy kicks and bites	Billy is removed from the situation for 2–5 minutes

Desirable Behaviour: Reward

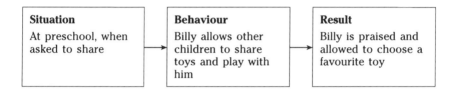

Situation	Behaviour	Result
At preschool, when asked to share	Billy allows other children to share toys and play with him	Billy is praised and allowed to choose a favourite toy

This is one possible explanation for Billy's aggressive behaviour. The situation, however, may be more complicated than this. An initial assessment is very important with any aggressive behaviour—look at the whole situation carefully in order to determine the child's possible motivation behind the behaviour.

For example:

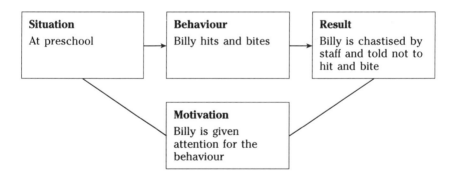

Situation	Behaviour	Result
At preschool	Billy hits and bites	Billy is chastised by staff and told not to hit and bite

Motivation
Billy is given attention for the behaviour

Billy is given attention for the inappropriate aggression. Another explanation may be that Billy does not know how to interact socially with other children. In this case, it will be necessary to design a program to introduce Billy gradually to more appropriate ways of interacting with others. This involves teaching Billy alternative ways of behaving through sharing and turn-taking games, modelling, introducing routines for some activities and giving Billy choices.

Bathtime

Some children appear to be afraid of water: they hate swimming, refuse to have a bath and hair-washing can be quite traumatic. It may take a long time to gradually increase some children's confidence around water. Other children may love water, but dislike the idea of someone invading their "personal space" and forcing close contact. It is also important to check that a child has not experienced a stressful incident at bathtime (for example, soap in the eyes, ducked under water, slipped in the bath, etc.).

Remember: Whenever a young child is playing around water, she *must* be closely supervised.

Intervention Strategies

Some of these may help build the child's confidence in bathing.

- Look beyond the problem behaviour to the situation in which it occurs. You may need to modify the situation as well as dealing with the behaviour.

- Initially, run only a few centimetres of water in the bath, and make sure that the water is lukewarm.
- Make the bath look pleasant with bubbles and some bath toys. Boats, plastic animals and cups for pouring are excellent toys.
- Allow the child to stand in the bath tub initially and sing songs about washing arms, legs, etc. Try to make a fun game out of bathtime.
- Encourage the child to enjoy water play at home. In summer, have a bucket of soapy water with toys or dolls to wash, play under the sprinkler, water the garden.
- Practise hair-washing on a doll in the bath, encourage the child to wash the dolly's hair.
- Use a gentle shampoo that won't sting the eyes.
- Wash hair quickly and rinse, praising the child for being cooperative.
- Try wetting hair and then rinsing by pouring water from a cup while the child is sitting in the bath. Some children do not feel safe lying back in the bath.
- Establish a routine time for bathing, maybe before a favourite TV show so that the child knows that there is something pleasant immediately after bathing.
- Encourage older children to model appropriate bathtime behaviour.
- Ensure that your expectations are realistic—wash hair as quickly as possible and keep hair short so that it is easy to wash.
- Touch your child at times other than hair-washing; for example, rub her head while she is watching TV to increase her tolerance of having her head touched.
- Praise the child for sitting still while her hair is washed and at the end of bathtime. Ignore as much as possible wriggling and squirming during bathing.

The aim is to encourage a more positive atmosphere at bathtime so that the experience becomes enjoyable and non-threatening for the child. This may involve not only teaching the child some coping skills such as closing eyes, holding breath, tolerating water on the face and assisting to wash herself, but also involve making the bathtime session more fun and enjoyable (toys in bath, bubblebath, games) and praising and reassuring the child continually.

Bedtime Tantrums

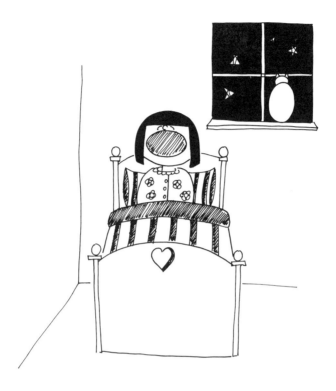

A bedtime tantrum can be a most effective way for a child to avoid an unwanted situation. This particular problem behaviour usually occurs at a time when most parents are vulnerable—they are tired after a long and exhausting day and are looking forward to some peace and quiet. Parents therefore often find it easier to give in to the child and allow her to get out of bed, play a while longer, or leave her room to watch more TV. A bedtime tantrum may also be the child's way of communicating that she is anxious or afraid, perhaps of the dark or of being left alone. If the child is afraid of the dark or of being alone, small changes in the environment may be sufficient to effect more appropriate bedtime behaviours. These changes may include installing a nightlight, having the child move into a room with a sibling, keeping the bedroom door open so that the child can hear other family members moving around or introducing a radio/tape player into the room to play quiet music. Parents should try to determine why the behaviour is occurring before implementing any management strategies. The child's bedroom should be made as comfortable and friendly as possible with familiar toys, books and favourite objects around, warm bedclothes and either a nightlight or some light from a hallway or another room. Parents should establish a bedtime routine and take a firm approach.

As with other behaviour-management programs, the key to success lies in remaining firm and consistent, not giving in to the child's demands and allowing the child to see who is in control. It is extremely important to determine precisely why the tantrum occurs and to modify the situation as much as possible.

Intervention Strategies

- Establish a regular, realistic bedtime.
- Establish a pattern of pre-bedtime behaviour: for example, offer a small drink; put pyjamas on; clean teeth; go to the toilet; kiss family goodnight; cuddle teddy and go to bed.
- If necessary, leave a nightlight on in the bedroom and hall.
- Have a pleasant bedtime activity ready—read a short story.
- Once the routine has been followed and the child is in bed, leave the room.
- Don't return to the room in response to a bedtime tantrum— this is reinforcing inappropriate behaviour. *Ignore* all tantrum behaviour.
- If the child leaves the bedroom, she should be returned immediately without fuss or comment.
- If the child has regular tantrums, it is important to child-proof her room—remove all breakable items and replace them with lots of soft toys for the child to throw around if she is really angry.
- Some parents have found it helpful to put a small catch on the child's door, thus ensuring that she remains in her room, and allowing parents to leave the scene rather than remain outside the door.
- If the child continually gets out of bed, stay outside the room for a while so that you can put her straight back into bed, giving her no opportunity to venture out of the bedroom.

For example, every night when Mary is put to bed, she begins to cry and scream until she is allowed to get up and watch TV.

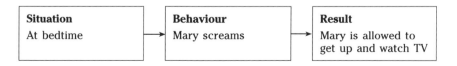

Situation	Behaviour	Result
At bedtime	Mary screams	Mary is allowed to get up and watch TV

Two-part Strategy

Undesirable Behaviour: Ignore

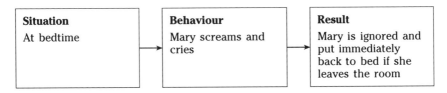

Situation	Behaviour	Result
At bedtime	Mary screams and cries	Mary is ignored and put immediately back to bed if she leaves the room

Desirable Behaviour: Reward

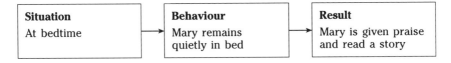

Situation	Behaviour	Result
At bedtime	Mary remains quietly in bed	Mary is given praise and read a story

By establishing a regular bedtime routine, and maintaining a firm and consistent approach, children eventually realise that bedtime is not an unpleasant experience.

Compulsive Behaviours: Opening and Closing Doors

A child may spend most of her time in repetitive stereotypical activities such as compulsively opening and closing cupboard doors. As with most ritualistic behaviours, this behaviour usually occurs when the child is not actively stimulated in some more appropriate way. Repetitive stereotypical activities are also common among children with limited communication and play skills, who do not have any more socially acceptable means of passing time. The aim of any management program is to reduce the severity or frequency of the behaviour, to teach the child skills to engage in more appropriate play and to restructure the child's environment so that the focus is upon more functional activities.

Intervention Strategies

- Initially, the aim is to restrict the child's opportunities to indulge in opening and closing doors.
- Use child-proof cupboard locks where appropriate.
- Teach the child alternative, functional play skills so that she can engage in more appropriate activities.
- Keep dangerous objects out of reach in high cupboards.
- Restrict the child to certain cupboards so that she is allowed to open the cupboard doors only in certain rooms. Gradually limit these further until she is allowed to open doors only in her own bedroom or the kitchen, and then only one cupboard in the room.
- When the child is restricted to one cupboard, ignore the behaviour and take her to this cupboard whenever she tries to open and close other doors. Store some plastic containers, wooden spoons or saucepan lids in this cupboard to keep the child amused in the kitchen. Put a sticker on the door of this cupboard so that the child knows which one is hers. You could do the same with one drawer. Show the child how to use these utensils in an imaginative way—encourage pretend play.
- Do not allow the child to play in any other cupboard or drawer at any time.
- Reward the child for not opening any other cupboards.
- Remember that it is not possible to entirely eliminate these obsessive, ritualistic behaviours—the aim is to reduce them to a manageable level.

Eating Problems

Problem behaviours involving food and eating vary among children, but are usually extremely disruptive to family harmony. Some children refuse to sit at the table, others refuse to feed themselves, other children are very fussy eaters, while others may be compulsive eaters and continually demand food or drink. Modifying a child's eating habits involves a strong commitment to a firm and consistent management program that may take months, even years, to successfully implement—eating habits cannot be changed overnight.

First, try to establish why the problem behaviour is occurring. Is the child seeking attention from parents, is she interested in food or not, is she able to sit for more than a few minutes, is she able to feed herself independently? All of these issues need to be considered and, if appropriate, addressed before implementing a program to change the behaviour.

Intervention Strategies

- At all times, remain cool and committed—your child will not starve.
- Look carefully at total nutrition for a full 24 hours before implementing any strategies—is the child really not eating anything nutritious or are you worried because she will not eat vegetables and fruit?
- Establish set mealtimes for the child and control snack times between these mealtimes.
- If possible, eat together as a family seated at the table.
- If the child makes mealtimes tense and unpleasant experiences for everyone, feed her first and, as behaviour improves, re-introduce the child to normal family mealtime routines.
- Establish the rule with the child that she has to be seated at the table to eat—if she leaves the table, then simply remove the food. If she returns to her seat, then replace the food—if she does not, then assume that she has finished. *Do not* chase after the child offering food and giving attention for inappropriate behaviour.
- If the child absolutely refuses to sit at the table, it may be necessary initially to "box the child in" for brief periods. Praise her for "good sitting" and gradually increase the time that she is expected to remain seated before she can leave the table.
- Establish sitting behaviour before moving to eating.
- Continue to introduce new foods in small portions and do not force the child to eat. Do not pay any attention to the child at this time, especially if she makes any attempt to try the new food. Go on talking with other family members and ignore the child's attempts to try the food. If the child does eat, you may simply say "Good girl", but do not make any fuss.
- Remove the child's plate without comment at the end of the meal.
- Praise the child for "good sitting".
- Avoid giving food between meals, and do not give junk food to a child who has refused her meal.
- If the child has refused a meal and is unable to last until the next meal, offer a small piece of fruit at mid-morning or mid-afternoon.

- Change the child's mealtime environment, for example, picnic in the park, eat outside—sometimes a child will eat food away from the home that she will not normally try.

For example, Billy refuses to sit at the table during mealtimes. He continually gets out of his seat and crawls under the table. He refuses to eat and prefers to snack during the day.

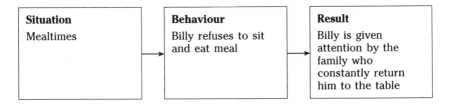

Situation	Behaviour	Result
Mealtimes	Billy refuses to sit and eat meal	Billy is given attention by the family who constantly return him to the table

Two-part Strategy

Undesirable Behaviour: Ignore

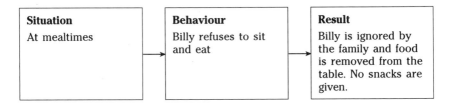

Situation	Behaviour	Result
At mealtimes	Billy refuses to sit and eat	Billy is ignored by the family and food is removed from the table. No snacks are given.

Desirable Behaviour: Reward

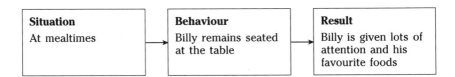

Situation	Behaviour	Result
At mealtimes	Billy remains seated at the table	Billy is given lots of attention and his favourite foods

Fussy Eaters

Some children are very fussy eaters and will happily survive on a diet of Coke, french fries and chocolate biscuits or hamburgers. Other children will eat only soft, mushy foods, sweet foods or savoury foods. Any program to change eating habits is, by necessity, a long-term one. The goal is to teach the child to try new foods, to tolerate different food tastes and textures and to establish a balanced diet. This may involve teaching some skills such as chewing, feeding independently and choosing for self.

Intervention Strategies

- When offering food, give only very small portions and offer one favourite food with something new and untried.
- Limit the amount of sweet or fast food the child is offered.
- Check that the child's food preference is not determined by texture, such as crunchy or sloppy food. If so, gradually introduce new textures.
- Do not overreact if the child begins to eat—this usually causes the child to down fork or spoon and refuse to continue. Try not to give attention until the food has been swallowed, then merely say, "Good girl".
- Don't offer between-meal snacks of junk food.
- Keep offering different foods.
- Keep records of the child's intake during the day—include both food and drink.
- Wean the child from the bottle—some children will not eat if they can fill up on milk.
- Try eating together as a family for one meal per day (usually dinner). Place about one spoonful of the food the family is eating on a plate in front of the child (for example, one piece of carrot, one small piece of meat, a couple of peas, etc.):

  do not feed the child or even encourage her to eat;

  give no attention, even if the child throws food on the floor— ignore it;

praise the child for "good sitting";

when the family has finished eating, then remove the child's plate and give her a small portion of the food she normally eats. Make no fuss/comment about the food left.

- Alternatively, place a small portion of the food the family is eating on the child's plate with some of her favourite food and ignore her eating. Remove the food left on her plate at the end of the meal and make no comments.

- Some food dislikes are not due to the actual flavour of the food—many children will refuse certain foods at home but quite happily eat the same things at preschool.

- A child may refuse to eat certain foods not because she particularly dislikes the food in question, but because she enjoys watching the reaction caused by her refusal to eat it. This is especially true of healthy foods such as vegetables because parents' reactions to refusal to eat these foods are usually strong.

- Ignore the child's power game—don't react to the refusal to eat.

- Put serving dishes on the table and give the child an empty plate. Let the child help herself. With a young child, offer help with food she is unable to serve herself.

- If the child chooses no food, then she is left with an empty plate. It usually takes only a couple of meals of looking at an empty plate while everyone else is enjoying food for the child to decide to select some food. This way, you are not forcing the child to eat, and if she eats nothing, it is her choice.

- Don't worry if the child misses a meal—she may feel hungry during the day. If the child becomes upset, offer a piece of fruit midway between the last meal and next, but *do not* offer sweets, biscuits or food left over from previous meal. The aim is not to overcome the child's hunger completely.

- Try to have set mealtimes with only a small snack in between meals. You must avoid establishing impossible eating habits for a family with everyone eating at different times.

- If the child demands biscuits, chocolate, chips etc. between meals, eliminate these items from the house completely so that they are no longer available to the child—this ensures that the child is not encouraged to snack between meals.

Gaze Avoidance

A child may actively avoid looking at a person when they are trying to communicate with her. A child may avoid looking a person in the

eye, but may look at the top of their head, beyond their face or at their body. Another child may look at a person, but it feels more as though she is looking through them. There is also evidence that some children suffer from a visual sensitivity that involves pain when looking directly at something or someone. Some children avoid looking directly at other people because it is too demanding and usually involves some unwanted social response.

Establishing eye contact is an important pre-language skill for children who have delayed language to learn. In order to successfully imitate, the child must be able to "look".

Intervention Strategies

These may help to improve the child's eye contact and general ability to look at objects and people.

- Some children may develop some form of visual sensitivity so that it appears to hurt them to look directly at a person or object. If this appears to be the case, it may be necessary to introduce the child gradually to new stimuli. Begin by expecting the child to look vaguely in the right direction of the person talking to her and reward the child for this. Gradually reward the child only if she looks more directly at the person, the upper torso, the head and eventually, aim for eye contact.

- Use objects with sounds or bright flashing lights or brightly coloured objects to gain the child's attention—for example, a biscuit or lolly. You must reward the child *immediately* by giving her the object.

- Put the object near to your face (in front of your chin) and reward the child if she gives you even fleeting eye contact.
- Placing the child's hand on your cheek may prompt her to look at you.
- Use a mirror with the child—she may become interested in looking at herself in the mirror and may also look at another person in the mirror.
- Ensure that the child is able to track successfully. If not, do some activities to improve tracking skills; for example,

    move sound toys from left to right in front of the child and see if she will follow the toy;

    tie a lolly to a piece of string and swing it from side to side and see if the child will follow the lolly.

- Play games with the child such as tickle games, bouncing on the knee. When you get to the end of the game, withhold the final action until the child looks at you.
- Blow bubbles—have the child pop the bubbles with her fingers. This is encouraging her to look.
- Play peek-a-boo games with the child and encourage eye contact.

Masturbation

Masturbation occurs quite frequently among young children and is a normal part of their growth and development. It is better to ignore the behaviour than to make a big fuss and give the child lots of attention. In some cases, it may be necessary to establish basic rules as to where and when masturbation may be allowed.

Intervention Strategies

- The less attention paid to masturbation, the less likely it is to occur frequently—give no attention and don't make comments to the child.
- Most young children are unable to distinguish between public and private places. If the behaviour is tolerated at home, then ensure that the child understands some basic rules—for example, only when the child is alone in the bedroom or bathroom. Treat all other places as public and masturbation as inappropriate in these areas.
- If masturbation is a problem when in the community, give the child something to carry which requires two hands.
- Dress the child in overalls when in public rather than dresses or shorts.
- If the child dislikes wearing clothes, *always* put the child in light underpants, even at home.

For example, Billy often begins to play with himself when out shopping or when the family visits grandparents.

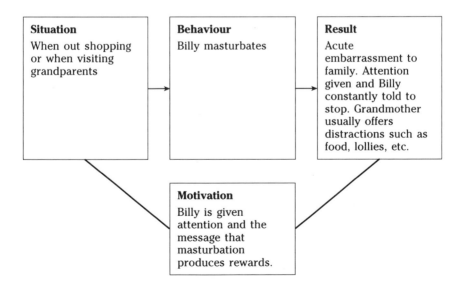

Situation	Behaviour	Result
When out shopping or when visiting grandparents	Billy masturbates	Acute embarrassment to family. Attention given and Billy constantly told to stop. Grandmother usually offers distractions such as food, lollies, etc.

Motivation
Billy is given attention and the message that masturbation produces rewards.

Management Strategy

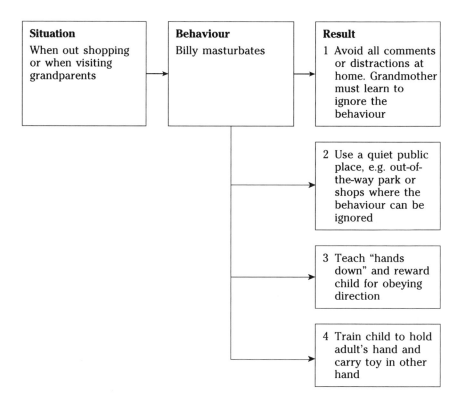

Situation	Behaviour	Result
When out shopping or when visiting grandparents	Billy masturbates	1 Avoid all comments or distractions at home. Grandmother must learn to ignore the behaviour
		2 Use a quiet public place, e.g. out-of-the-way park or shops where the behaviour can be ignored
		3 Teach "hands down" and reward child for obeying direction
		4 Train child to hold adult's hand and carry toy in other hand

Obsessive Behaviours and Obsession with Objects

Many children may use obsessions as an attempt to provide some sort of order to a world that appears extremely disordered and chaotic to them. Initially, if possible, determine the function that the behaviour achieves. It may also be possible to look at how the obsessive behaviours developed. This information will assist when developing a systematic approach to modify the behaviour. The child should be taught new skills—to play with objects and toys in a more appropriate manner; to go places without becoming involved in certain rituals; to expand interests; and to accept different people, places and events. With some children, it is not always clear why they engage in obsessive behaviours. Many obsessions cannot be eliminated—the aim should be to decrease the time spent on obsessions and also to have some control over when the child engages in obsessive behaviour.

Intervention Strategies

- Increase the child's ability to communicate and play appropriately. Once the child knows how to play appropriately with objects, the desire and time to engage in obsessive behaviours should decrease.
- Rituals and obsessions tend to increase in intensity over time. If you are aware of the child beginning to engage in obsessive/ritualistic behaviours, immediately try to reduce or eliminate them before they become too entrenched.
- Encourage the child to gradually accept changes in the pattern of her obsession in order to modify the obsessive behaviour to a more acceptable level (see Part D).
- Restrict the child's opportunities to engage in these behaviours.
- It is not possible to eliminate all obsessions entirely—the aim is to reduce the behaviours to a manageable level so they do not interfere with everyday life.
- Reduce the number of objects that are involved in the child's obsession gradually (for example, the number of trains or cars to be lined up).

- Limit the amount of time that the child is allowed to engage in obsessive play.
- Use obsessions as a reward for activities completed; for example, allow the child to line up cars for 5 minutes after she has completed a specific task.
- Use obsession to overcome a particular difficulty; for example, if the child continually gets out of her car seat, then allow her to hold her piece of string or other obsession while she remains in her seat. As soon as she undoes her seatbelt, then take away her obsession object until she is behaving appropriately. Remove the string or other object as soon as you stop the car.
- The important thing to remember with an obsessive child is to ensure that you are in control in most situations, *not* the child.
- If you remove or successfully eliminate a child's particular obsession, the chances are she will find another one—it is therefore important to look closely at an obsession before attempting to modify it, because the new obsession may end up to be worse than the original.
- When the child is engaged in an obsessive activity, briefly and occasionally disrupt the child in order to help build up her tolerance for change.
- Provide less than perfectly matched materials—for example, irregular shaped blocks, cars and trucks of different size and type so that the child's obsession does not remain too specific. Gradually, the obsession should fade away.
- Obsessional objects such as a piece of string may provide the individual with comfort in stressful situations. Rather than forcefully removing the object, encourage the child to release the object voluntarily at times when you require her attention to complete a task—for example, Mary must put her string next to her plate during mealtimes. This may help prevent tantrum behaviours if the child is forced to give up the object without knowing if or when it will be returned.
- If a child is obsessed with carrying one object in particular, limit its availability to certain times of the day—it may not be appropriate to hold it during lunch or during an activity that is best done with two hands.
- Show the child how to play with the objects of obsession more appropriately.
- Encourage the child to voluntarily hand over objects of obsession at certain times. Do not snatch the objects from the child, as this will probably lead to distress and anxiety and tantrum behaviours. The child also learns not to trust you.

Screaming

Screaming may be used as an attention-seeking device, as a way to avoid an unwanted situation or to communicate a want or a need. Some children may impulsively scream for no apparent reason other than the fact that they like to hear the sound of their own voices. Whatever the motivation behind the problem behaviour, it is frustrating and embarrassing for other family members. Screaming should be understood as having a communicative function. Therefore look closely at the situation in which the behaviour occurs, and develop alternative means of communication as well as making any necessary changes to the child's environment.

Intervention Strategies

- Ignore screaming as much as possible when it occurs so as not to reinforce the behaviour, *but* determine the function of the behaviour.
- Look at the situation in which screaming occurs.
- Screaming may be reinforced by enjoyment of the underlying effect—for example, the sound of the voice echoing in a covered car park or bathroom.
- Screaming may be a habit that has previously obtained a reaction.
- Encourage quiet, appropriate behaviour in particular situations— keep these situations short and immediately reward quiet behaviour.

- Screaming may be used to obtain a desired object—anticipate the request and give the item at the first sound. This limits screaming and may be shaped into an appropriate asking sound. Introduce more appropriate ways for the child to request objects—for example, pointing, taking hand, labelling object verbally.
- Screaming may be an attempt to avoid a certain activity or object. Model and pattern a headshake while saying "No"—tell me, "No". This may lead to an acceptable alternative to screaming.
- Screaming may occur through frustration and anger. This should be acknowledged, and if necessary, a designated place where screaming is allowed should be set up—"If you must scream, you go to the laundry/bathroom,"—physically assist, if necessary. Encourage the child to learn how to choose between objects— for example, "Do you want milk or juice?"

For example, whenever Billy wants to avoid a certain situation, he screams loudly and continuously.

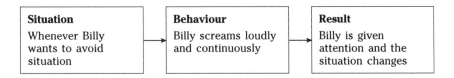

Situation	Behaviour	Result
Whenever Billy wants to avoid situation	Billy screams loudly and continuously	Billy is given attention and the situation changes

Management Strategy

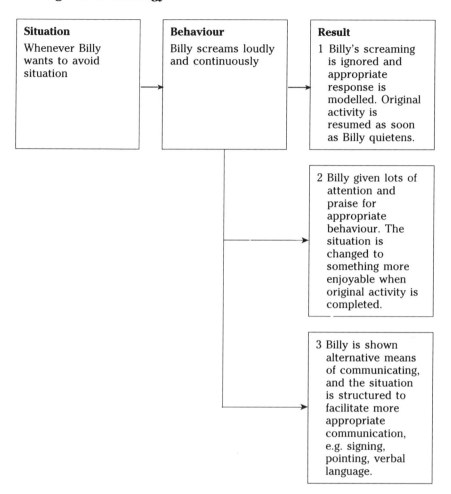

Situation	Behaviour	Result
Whenever Billy wants to avoid situation	Billy screams loudly and continuously	1 Billy's screaming is ignored and appropriate response is modelled. Original activity is resumed as soon as Billy quietens.
		2 Billy given lots of attention and praise for appropriate behaviour. The situation is changed to something more enjoyable when original activity is completed.
		3 Billy is shown alternative means of communicating, and the situation is structured to facilitate more appropriate communication, e.g. signing, pointing, verbal language.

Problem behaviours, such as screaming, will never be successfully eliminated until the child is shown alternative and more useful ways of communicating effectively. It is not enough to simply ignore the behaviour—this will only lead to continued frustration. The child should be discouraged from screaming, but at the same time, taught appropriate communicative behaviour to elicit wants and needs.

Self-abuse

Self-abusive behaviours cannot be ignored. However, keep attention to a minimum and make attempts to provide the child with less

harmful ways to release anger and frustration. As discussed previously, it is essential to determine the function of the behaviour—what is the message that the child is attempting to communicate? Check that the child is not in pain and unable to communicate in a more appropriate manner:—it may be a headache, earache, toothache, etc. It is important to eliminate this possibility before implementing any behaviour-management program.

Intervention Strategies

- Give minimal attention to the child to avoid reinforcing the behaviour.
- Self-abuse is best managed from a preventative point of view. This may involve redirecting the child to another activity or situation as soon as the child begins to self-abuse, rearranging the situation that is causing anxiety in the child and encouraging her to express her feelings in more socially acceptable ways.
- Look at when the behaviour occurs and, if possible, change the situation.
- Some children self-abuse because they are being overstimulated by sensations in the environment. It may be necessary to decrease the amount of sensory stimulation that the child is exposed to.
- Distract the child from the situation—redirect the child.

- Positively reinforce the child for appropriate behaviour—do this constantly and consistently.
- Calling out aloud "No" may divert the child's attention away from the behaviour.
- Avoid physical restraint whenever possible—this may only aggravate the situation.
- Withhold all possible attention from the child while she is engaging in self-abusive behaviour.
- Give the child an alternative—a pillow to bang her head on, a soft toy to bite.
- Some children have an abnormal tolerance of pain and may hurt themselves without feeling excessive pain—it is important to understand this when working with children who self-abuse.
- A child may self-abuse in certain situations. If the situation cannot be changed, it may be necessary to provide support to the child in these situations—for example, it may be easier to give in to certain obsessions to avoid stressing the child, to complete unfamiliar tasks at quiet times and to constantly reward the child to keep anxiety levels low.
- Inform all people who are involved with the child, and discuss strategies with them whenever you implement any specific program to decrease self-abusive behaviour that is dangerous to the child's health and well-being.
- If a child engages in self-abusive behaviour regularly, it is advisable to contact experts who will be able to assist in designing and implementing a behaviour-management program, encourage alternative communication and remove pressure from the child by changing her environment.

For example, whenever Billy is irritable or does not get his own way, he bangs his head repeatedly.

Situation	Behaviour	Result
Billy gets out of car after shopping and is irritable	Walks into lounge and repeatedly bangs head on coffee table	Billy is given lots of attention

By changing the situation, it may be possible to distract Billy away from self-abusive behaviours.

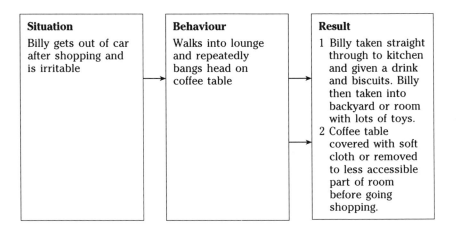

For example, Billy objects when unfamiliar people visit the house.

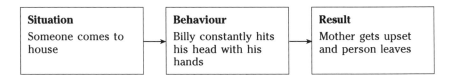

Billy's space has been invaded and he is stressed by the unfamiliar person's presence. Billy requires reassurance that there is nothing threatening to him in the situation.

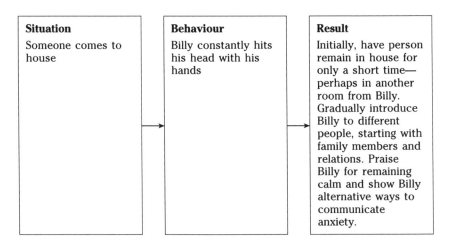

In the example above, if Billy has difficulty coping with unfamiliar people, places or events, it may take time to increase his tolerance and decrease his anxiety. This may involve showing him ways of coping by introducing changes gradually and positively, maintaining some consistency and constancy, and also teaching Billy other ways to decrease his anxiety (for example, leave the room, hold familiar adult's hand) and communicate his fear.

Shopping

Taking young children shopping is often a difficult and stressful activity for parents and children. The children may become bored, frustrated and tired, and will express this through some inappropriate behaviour. Some children become anxious and fearful in big shopping centres, others may dislike the bright lights, loud noises and large crowds usually associated with modern centres and shopping malls.

Some children with autism may be hypersensitive to sound, vision, taste or touch, and so may receive distorted sensory messages. Large centres are confusing and frightening places for these children. We need to look closely at possible reasons for the anxiety and stress that some children exhibit while shopping. They may be taught more appropriate ways to behave, alternative ways to communicate their feelings and also ways of increasing their enjoyment of the experience.

As stated previously, it is not enough to modify the tantrum behaviour in the immediate context, but it is important to look at the overall function—to educate the child and change the environment to decrease or eliminate the problem.

Intervention Strategies

- Practice walking with the child holding hands before going shopping—lots of "walking practice" at the park or around the block.
- Initially, take the child shopping for a brief time—approximately 5–10 minutes.
- Choose a time when the shops are not busy.
- Choose a small shopping centre, a row of small shops or a small supermarket.
- Gradually extend the time spent shopping, but still go to a small centre during a quiet period.
- Choose only a few items to buy initially and gradually extend the shopping list.
- Ignore any tantrum behaviour.
- Reward the child at the end of the shopping trip for good behaviour—for example, chips, a drink, ice cream, or a ride.
- Sometimes, it may be necessary to reward the child throughout the outing—every 2 minutes with a sultana, lolly or happy stamp (depending on what motivates the child). Remember, reward only for appropriate behaviour and do not reward the child for negative or tantrum behaviour—choose a reward that is meaningful to the child.
- Give the child something to carry—actively involve the child in the shopping task.
- If the child is obsessed by certain toys, foods, rides, etc., avoid these sections while training the child to remain with you.
- Talk with the child—discuss what you are buying, give the child a copy of the shopping list to hold and constantly praise child for appropriate behaviour, for helping, for walking, for holding hands, etc.
- Try to ignore comments or looks from other shoppers when the child is displaying inappropriate behaviours. There is no easy way out—merely smile, develop a thick skin, ignore it, but persevere and remain consistent with the child.

For example, Billy would scream and constantly drop to the floor, refusing to walk, whenever his mother took him shopping at the local shopping centre.

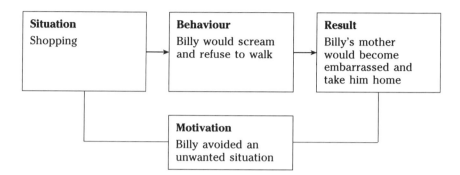

Billy behaves inappropriately in order to avoid an unpleasant situation. He may not feel comfortable at the shopping centre and he may be overstimulated by all the visual and auditory effects. Once Billy's mother is aware of the problem, she can take steps to modify the situation, the behaviour and the results.

Once Billy is more comfortable and relaxed in this situation, his mother may gradually extend the time spent shopping and also eventually generalise the situation to other centres. The emphasis is always on increasing Billy's tolerance slowly and positively in a non-threatening way.

Sleeping in Parents' Bed

Children's sleeping habits vary greatly, as do parents' expectations of their children's behaviour at bedtime. Some parents accept the fact that their child prefers to sleep with them, other parents find such behaviour unacceptable. There is no hard and fast rule about where a child should sleep—it is a matter of personal choice. However, remember that eventually most parents prefer their child to

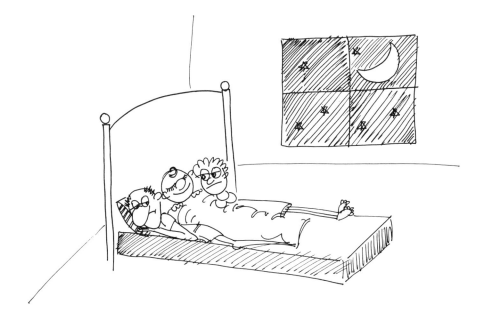

sleep in her own room. When that time arrives, it is good to have some strategies to help the child make the transition smoothly and painlessly.

Intervention Strategies

These are merely ideas that may help to break the child's sleeping habits.

- Look closely at why the child is refusing to sleep in her own bed—deal with physical and emotional issues such as not enough blankets, fear of the dark, the child not feeling well, lack of security, and see if behaviour improves before implementing behaviour-management strategies.
- Alter the parents' bedroom arrangements so that the child cannot climb into the bed where she usually does.
- Alter the child's bedroom so that it is less easy for the child to leave the bed or cot.
- The best time to implement strategies is the night following a break in routine—for example, after a holiday, or after the child has been staying at grandparents overnight.
- When the child attempts to climb into the parents' bed, take her immediately back to her own room.

- Offer the child a small drink, check her nappy and change it if necessary, toilet the child, check for temperature, add or remove a blanket. Say goodnight, tuck her in and return to your own room.
- If the child enters parents' room again, return her immediately to her own room without comment. Repeat as often as necessary. Remember to return the child immediately, not after a cuddle for half an hour or a story.
- Do not stay with the child to pat her off to sleep or allow her to play.
- Keep eye contact to a minimum.
- Remain consistent with your approach, and be prepared for a couple of sleepless nights before your child gives up and remains in her own bed.
- If all else fails, consider buying the child a water bed—some children enjoy and find comfort in the enclosed, moulding feeling and gentle movement of a water bed.
- This problem behaviour may be a difficult one for parents to address successfully. Professional advice and assistance is available to families who do not feel confident about tackling the issue of their child's sleeping habits. It is worth discussing the problem with an expert before taking steps to move the child back to her own bed—the expert may come up with a simple solution or have some different ideas to try.
- The desire to sleep in the parents' bed often develops gradually after a child has been sick and parents have kept the child in with them in order to monitor her. When the child is well and it comes time to move back to her own bed, the child decides that she prefers the present arrangement and refuses to budge. It may be preferable to avoid the habit in the first instance by monitoring the child in her own room. Make sure that the child's room is warm and inviting, that she has plenty of familiar and favourite objects around her and that the room has a nightlight.

Spinning Objects

A child may continually spin objects because she does not know how to play with toys and objects in an age-appropriate manner. However, the majority of children who continually spin objects derive some form of self-stimulation from the activity. In order to obtain a clear picture, we need to look closely at the pattern of the

behaviour to determine why the child repetitively self-stimulates, when it occurs and what is associated with it. Obsessions, such as spinning objects, generally decrease as the child's interests broaden and she is offered alternative ways to remain stimulated and busy.

Intervention Strategies

- Show the child how to use toys more constructively—for example, turn the car over and show the child how to push it along.
- Praise the child for playing appropriately—for example, "Good girl. You are pushing the car."
- Encourage the child to develop many different, creative ways to play with each toy or object.
- If an object has been designed for a specific purpose, show the child how to use it appropriately—for example, a lid was designed to screw onto the jar, *not* to repetitively spin.

- If the child consistently chooses the same object to spin and it appears to interfere with more appropriate play, put the object away for a while.
- Give the child toys that are difficult to spin.
- Keep a special super-spinning toy to use as a reward, but this should be kept under adults' control and not be kept with the other toys.
- If the function of the behaviour appears to be to alleviate stress or to calm the child, then there are times when she should be allowed to spin objects—for example, after tiring therapy sessions, when both parent and child need time to relax. This is only for short periods, and at the same time attempts should be made to teach the child other, more appropriate ways to relax.
- Use the child's obsession with spinning as a teaching device— its uses are endless and it is extremely motivating for the child— for example, "When you have completed this activity, you may have your special spinner."
- If you use the child's obsession with spinning as a reward, you must put a time limit on how long the child can spin—for example, 2–5 minutes. The spinning behaviour should remain under adult control.
- Check whether the child's problem is self-stimulating or is being used to block out overwhelming stimuli in the child's environment, such as light or sound.

For example, Billy always turns every toy over until he can find one part of it to spin, or he attempts to spin the whole toy. If he is unable to spin the toy, he becomes agitated and upset.

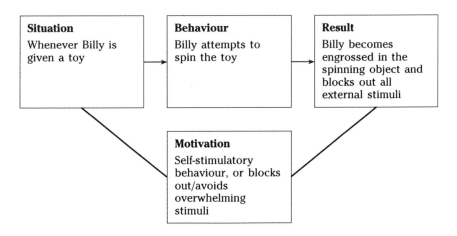

| **Situation** | **Behaviour** | **Result** |
| Whenever Billy is given a toy | Billy attempts to spin the toy | Billy becomes engrossed in the spinning object and blocks out all external stimuli |

Motivation
Self-stimulatory behaviour, or blocks out/avoids overwhelming stimuli

Two-part Strategy

Undesirable Behaviour: Remove Rewards

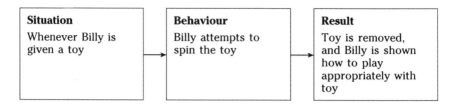

Situation	Behaviour	Result
Whenever Billy is given a toy	Billy attempts to spin the toy	Toy is removed, and Billy is shown how to play appropriately with toy

Desirable Behaviour: Give Rewards

Situation	Behaviour	Result
Whenever Billy is given a toy	Billy plays appropriately	Billy is praised and encouraged to continue. He may be allowed a few minutes to spin later.

Once again, it is important to initially determine the communicative intent of the behaviour. Is it that the child does not have the skills to play with objects in an appropriate manner, is it to relieve stress and anxiety or is it to relieve boredom? These are just a few possibilities, but all require careful management and some educational training. Show the child alternative and additional ways to play. Change her lifestyle to eliminate or decrease stressful situations and teach her ways to deal with them when they occur.

Stripping-off Clothing

Some children dislike the feel of heavy clothing against their bodies. Others have an abnormal reaction to changes in temperature and do not ever appear to feel cold. These children may continually strip off their clothing because they prefer to run around naked. Other children may react to the response they obtain from embarrassed family members when they strip off in public. These are all possible functions for the problem behaviour of stripping.

Intervention Strategies

- Look at when the child strips off clothing—it may be because she does not like the feel or smell of certain clothes against

her body. You may need to play lots of activities involving the senses—for example tactile games, guessing the object from touch or feel or taste or smell, etc.

- Use a mild washing power with no perfume.
- Gradually desensitise the child to the feel of fabric by towelling her gently, then more vigorously after bathing.
- Put the child in clothes that are difficult to remove, such as overalls.
- In hot weather, keep the child in at least a nappy or pants even at home.
- Use a belt to keep jeans up and buckle the belt at the back so that the child is unable to reach it.
- If the child prefers to be naked, gradually build up the child's tolerance to wearing clothes by adding more layers over time; that is, the child may wear just underpants, then add an under-shirt, then a T-shirt, shorts, etc.
- Try to buy some clothing that fastens at the back with buttons or zippers. Some clothing can be worn back to front to make it difficult to remove.

- If a child strips off her clothing, put the clothes back on *immediately* and reinforce by giving attention to others wearing clothes, commenting on how nice they look, etc.
- If a child continues to strip, *always* replace her clothes with minimal attention so that she learns that it is not appropriate to strip and that she does not receive any attention for the behaviour.
- Try to distract the child by offering different activities as soon as the clothes have been replaced. Redirection may help the child to forget about the stripping as long as the new activity is motivating and interesting.
- Reward the child for wearing clothes—give her something she likes to do and encourage alternative appropriate behaviours.
- Let the child choose her favourite clothes to wear—if necessary, buy clothes that have logos or pictures of favourite cartoon or TV show characters on them.
- When the child has new clothes or shoes, rub them against her body, feet or hands so that she becomes familiar with the smell and feel of the clothing.
- As with all problem behaviours, be consistent and firm in your management of the problem behaviour—always replace the clothes.

Teeth-cleaning

Some children find the task of cleaning their teeth extremely distressing and intrusive. They may not like the sensation of the toothbrush rubbing against their teeth and mouth; some children have sensitive palates and will gag at objects placed in the mouth or on the tongue. Other children may dislike the taste of the toothpaste.

Intervention Strategies

These may help to build up child's tolerance to teeth-cleaning.

- Use Colgate Junior toothpaste or a salt/saline solution that has a mild taste.
- If the child is obsessed with certain cartoon characters (such as Thomas the Tank Engine, Donald Duck, Big Bird), try to find a toothbrush with a picture of the favourite character. If this is not available, make your own by placing a sticker or picture on the child's toothbrush.
- Initially, introduce the child to the idea of cleaning her teeth through functional play—for example, have the child brush Teddy's teeth.

- Practise less intrusive activities with the mouth; start by dipping your finger into something the child likes the taste of, like peanut butter, and rubbing this on the child's teeth. Try this with a few different flavours, then introduce toothpaste still only using the finger—keep praising the child for allowing you to touch her teeth and reward her with a favourite activity when finished. (Don't reward with food as you do not want the child to develop the habit of eating after teeth-cleaning.) It may be best to try this activity at routine times such as morning and before bed, but not in the bathroom where it will be associated with unpleasant teeth-cleaning.
- When the child is comfortable with having you brush with your finger, introduce an implement—a cotton bud works well—and "brush" with a small amount of toothpaste on this. Practise this for a few days, keep praising the child and do something pleasant afterwards.
- Now for the toothbrush! Ensure that it has soft bristles and is a junior size. It may help to take the child shopping for a new "special" one with a cartoon character on it. Put a small amount of paste on the brush and either brush the teeth gently yourself or hold your hand over the child's hand on the brush and assist her to brush.

- Give the child a spare toothbrush to play with during the day.
- Brush the child's teeth lightly and briefly to begin with, and then reward the child for opening her mouth.
- As the child begins to tolerate teeth-cleaning, increase the length of time in brushing but not the pressure—continue to brush lightly.
- Encourage the child to hold the toothbrush, to put toothpaste on the brush and to complete the task independently—offer physical assistance as required.
- If the child resists, position yourself behind the child for most effective management—you can hold the child's head against your stomach if she remains uncooperative.
- Have the child stand on a booster chair so that she can see in the mirror; this also makes it more difficult for the child to escape.
- Some children respond well to a star or sticker chart for teeth-cleaning.
- Help your child to practise teeth-cleaning on a doll and make it fun.
- Play games in a mirror looking at and touching teeth.
- Older brothers and sisters can model good teeth-cleaning behaviours and may give your child someone else to practise on.
- You need to abandon the toothbrush before beginning this program and during the early stages, when using your finger and cotton bud, in order to make a fresh start. If you are worried about your child's oral hygiene during this time, try to limit sweet, sticky foods; offer a piece of apple after mealtimes and give your child plenty of water to drink after eating.
- Give the child lots of water to drink rather than juice or a fizzy drink—the water contains fluoride, which will strengthen the child's teeth and help prevent cavities.
- If the child requires dental work, either look for a sympathetic and knowledgeable paediatric dentist or go to a recognised dental clinic attached to a teaching hospital, a clinic that is experienced in treating young children with special needs.

Throwing Objects

A child may throw objects for a number of different reasons. If a child continually throws objects, assess the potential communicative functions of the problem behaviour, and use this information

to develop appropriate and successful intervention strategies. It may be to gain attention, to avoid an unwanted situation or because of frustration. Some children have to be shown how to play appropriately with toys and other objects.

Intervention Strategies

These are merely ideas that may help in changing inappropriate throwing.

- Ensure that the child knows how to play appropriately with toys—if not, show her how to play in different ways.
- Give the child a limited choice of toys to play with.
- Do not have too many toys within reach of the child—she will only become overwhelmed and not concentrate on anything.
- Once the child has chosen a certain toy, encourage her to spend some time playing with it before she puts it away and chooses another.
- Give attention to appropriate play behaviour.
- Check that toys are age-appropriate for the child—are they too difficult for the child's current level of functioning or perhaps too simple?
- Check the situation in which the throwing behaviour occurs— what was happening before the throwing took place?

- If the child appears to be throwing because she is bored, rather than eliminating the behaviour it may be more appropriate to teach the child ways of signalling that she needs a break or a change of activity.
- Is the throwing a form of self-stimulation—does the child continually throw certain objects into the air, under the table or over the fence? If this is the case, it may be necessary to remove the objects for a while.
- If a child obsessively throws or posts objects, it may not be possible to eliminate the problem behaviour entirely. The initial aim may be to decrease the behaviour and to maintain some control over when the child engages in it. Whenever the child engages in inappropriate throwing or posting, she should be taken to her room and told, "No throwing outside, you can throw in your room." Before doing this, it is essential to check the child's room, remove all breakable objects and add some soft toys, pillows, soft balls (ping pong balls, nerf balls) that the child can safely throw around without causing any damage. The child is left in her room with no verbal directions and with the door closed for approximately 5 minutes. The child is not given any attention, her throwing is ignored, but at the same time limits are set as to where and for how long she can engage in the behaviour.
- Concurrently with any behaviour-management program, the child should be given alternative, more socially acceptable ways to play, be given opportunities to participate in other activities and be kept busy and stimulated.
- If throwing occurs occasionally, it may be best to ignore the behaviour—give no eye contact and no attention.
- Praise other children for playing appropriately—encourage appropriate role models.
- Tell the child to, "Pick up the toy"; physically prompt when necessary to give minimal attention.
- Return the child to the previous activity immediately after she has picked up the thrown object—throwing should not be used as a means of avoiding an unwanted situation.
- Teach appropriate throwing through games involving balls, bean bags and balloons.

For example, whenever other children are present, or whenever Billy wishes to avoid a situation, he will pick up the nearest object/ toy and throw it. We need to determine whether Billy is throwing because he wants to avoid the situation, because he is excited or because he does not have appropriate social skills to relate to the other children.

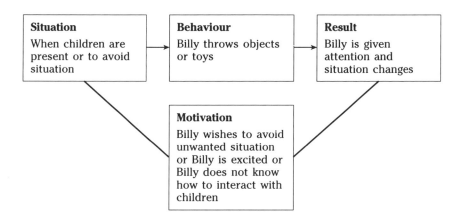

Two-part Strategy

Undesirable Behaviour: Ignore

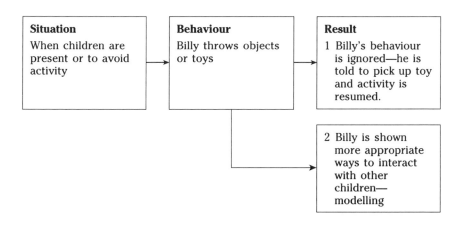

Desirable Behaviour: Reward

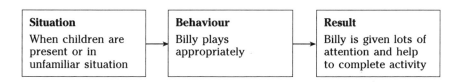

Toe-walking

Toe-walking is a problem that occurs quite frequently among children with special needs. Children may toe-walk for a variety of reasons, and there is no quick method to successfully eliminate the problem. Most children eventually grow out of the behaviour or forget to do it when they are stimulated and busy. This behaviour is best ignored.

Intervention Strategies

- Behaviour is difficult to eliminate and is often best ignored.
- It is more obvious when the child is not wearing shoes or has on soft slippers. Encourage the child to keep her shoes on and ensure that she wears firmer, more supportive shoes.
- The child will not hurt herself toe-walking and it does not interfere with her learning.
- Have the child walk along low brick walls placing one foot in front of the other and balancing with minimal support. To keep her balance, the child is more inclined to walk flat-footedly.
- Take the child on walks over hilly terrain or use climbing equipment at the park.
- Play stamping games and encourage flat-foot and heel-walking.
- Buy "high top" shoes or gym boots that support the ankle and make it more difficult to toe-walk.
- Seek a physiotherapist's advice, and follow simple exercises or massage routines to stretch ligaments in the heel and behind knees.

- Toe-walking may occur in children who have some sensitivity to touch, that is, the pressure of placing the whole foot on the ground may cause overstimulation. If this is the case, play lots of tactile activities with the child involving touching and feeling materials of different textures.

Toileting

These strategies on toileting have been included in this section even though, in the majority of cases, toileting should not be classified as a problem behaviour, but rather as a skill yet to be learned by the young child. All children develop skills at different rates, so do not become anxious and concerned if your child is still in nappies at 3 or 4, while your best friend's child of the same age is completely toilet-trained.

Many parents immediately become anxious as soon as the world "toileting" is mentioned. Most children can be successfully toilet-trained with a minimum of fuss and anxiety. The secret to any successful toileting program is to establish a routine, remain relaxed and don't nag the child.

A number of strategies are listed below that may assist you when you feel that you are ready and, most importantly, *your child* is ready to begin toilet-training.

Intervention Strategies

- For at least the first year and well into the second year, children have no real voluntary bladder or bowel control.
- A child cannot be properly toilet-trained until the central nervous system has matured enough so that the child can control the appropriate muscles.
- Begin toilet-training by introducing the toddler to the potty. Encourage the child to sit on the potty with or without her nappy on. Keep the time short and the atmosphere relaxed.
- Take the child to the toilet at regular intervals—at least every hour and about 20 minutes after mealtimes or after having a drink. Encourage the child to sit for 1–3 minutes.
- Ensure that the child is seated comfortably—use a plastic inner seat to help child feel secure about sitting, also a small stool or stacked phone books to support the feet in a sitting position.
- Ignore accidents—never punish a child for having an accident. Change the child quietly and without comment. Save your attention for when the child has been successful.
- Praise lavishly for "good sitting".
- Don't force the child to sit on the potty or toilet—if the child is not yet ready to sit happily, then take a break and try again a few days later.
- Most children like the idea of being a "big boy" or a "big girl". They also like copying—so it may help to let them watch Mum or Dad as role models.
- Don't stop a child from having a drink in the evening—although too much fluid may lead to a wet mattress. Try to monitor fluid intake, and ensure that if the child has had a drink with dinner or after dinner that she also sits on the potty or toilet before bed.
- Dress the child in clothes that are easy to remove.
- Constipation can lead to painful bowel movements and make a child fear toileting, so ensure that the child's diet contains plenty of roughage, fruit, vegetables and fluids.
- Some boys prefer to stand to urinate rather than sit—that's OK. Just remember that the boy who stands will be less accurate than the child who sits.

- Keep all toileting routine relaxed and straightforward—don't talk a lot about "trying". Don't nag. Just encourage the child to sit on the potty or toilet for 1–3 minutes, praise her for remaining seated, change pants if necessary, then wash hands and return to previous activity. The whole idea of toilet-training is to help the child become independent and recognise her own need to use the toilet.
- Remember that all young children have accidents, especially when they are busily engrossed in an enjoyable activity.
- When out in the community, make sure that you are aware of where the public toilets are. Encourage the child to generalise her toileting skills to different toilets.
- A tangible reward such as a sticker, stamp, lolly or piece of chocolate (depending on the child's preference) may be given immediately after the child produces something in the toilet.
- All children suffer occasional setbacks when they are ill or upset. A new baby in the house may cause a young child to regress temporarily.
- The toilet flushing may be frightening to some children and rewarding to others—establish the child's preference and make allowances.
- Learning to use the toilet makes a child feel important and successful. We want to encourage these feelings, so ensure that you never let the child see your frustration and anger while they are still trying to master this important task.

NB: If there is any history of urinary infection in the family and the child appears to be suffering pain or discomfort, consult a urologist. Do this before attempting to toilet-train the child.

For example, Billy refuses to sit on the potty and constantly urinates in his pants. Billy may be frightened of the potty or he may have no idea what is expected of him. He may also like the attention he receives when he is changed.

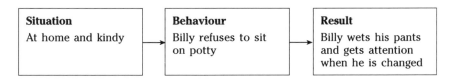

Situation	Behaviour	Result
At home and kindy	Billy refuses to sit on potty	Billy wets his pants and gets attention when he is changed

Two-part Strategy

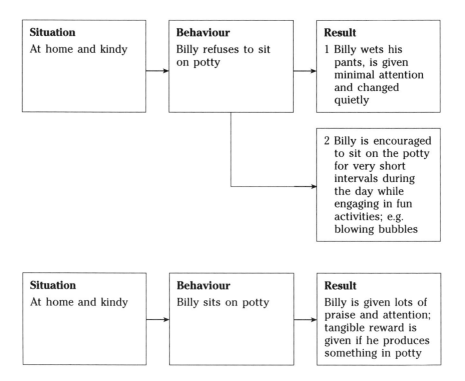

Situation	Behaviour	Result
At home and kindy	Billy refuses to sit on potty	1 Billy wets his pants, is given minimal attention and changed quietly
		2 Billy is encouraged to sit on the potty for very short intervals during the day while engaging in fun activities; e.g. blowing bubbles

Situation	Behaviour	Result
At home and kindy	Billy sits on potty	Billy is given lots of praise and attention; tangible reward is given if he produces something in potty

Travelling by Car

The majority of young children enjoy travelling by car; they find pleasure in the car movement, are happy to experience new situations and they do not mind sitting in a car seat or seatbelt. However, some children display very difficult behaviour if they are required to travel by car. They may refuse to remain in their car seat, they may unfasten the seatbelt, they may continually remove their clothing and may become extremely upset and agitated if an unfamiliar route is taken. These problem behaviours are impossible to ignore in the car, and some children seem to understand this. They actively manipulate the situation so that they are given attention or whatever else they want. It is important neither to accept these behaviours nor to make compromises. For safety reasons, a child must remain belted into a car seat or booster seat even if severe tantrum behaviour occurs.

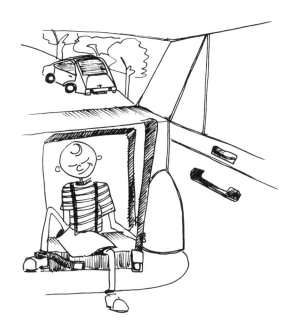

Intervention Strategies

- Use a booster seat and, if necessary, a harness if the child removes her seatbelt.
- If the child still manages to get out of her seatbelt, then go back to the baby car seat.
- Place the seatbelt buckle underneath the booster seat or car seat out of reach of the child.
- As soon as the child unclips the seatbelt, stop the car and do up the belt, making no comments and giving no eye contact. The child may have *accidentally* pushed the right button, so it is important not to reinforce the inappropriate behaviour.
- If the child removes her seatbelt and gets out of her seat, *immediately* stop the car. Reposition the child and refasten the seatbelt, saying, "Seatbelt on." Restart the car and proceed. You may need to practise this in a quiet area where you can stop suddenly and as often as necessary.
- Give lots of attention and praise to the child when she is sitting appropriately.
- If the child does not respond to praise and attention or if she has become obsessed with getting out of her seat, you may need to consider more stringent measures such as:

taping over belt buckle;

have her wear ski mittens securely fastened for a short time;

reward the child with lollies, biscuits, etc., for sitting appropriately.

- Have lots of objects of interest to the child in the car such as toys, books, etc.

- Give the child an object or toy to hold while in the car. Keep this toy for use only in the car. If the child removes the belt or gets out of the seat, stop the car and remove the toy. Put the child back in her seat and return the toy—as you return the toy, say "Good sitting in the car." The toy is removed every time the child unfastens the seatbelt and is returned every time the child sits appropriately.

- Use a cassette player with children's tapes and songs to distract the child's attention away from the problem behaviours. If necessary, use this as a reward. Make car trips as pleasant and interesting as possible—sing along with tapes, reward the child and point out things of interest to her along the way.

- Carry biscuits and drinks for emergencies.

- Ensure that the child-proof locks are on, and in summer, invest in sunshields for the side windows.

- Have another adult or sibling travel in the back with the child. If the child attempts to remove her belt, have the other person refasten it without comment. Use rewards such as jelly beans or biscuits for good sitting, and praise the child for sitting appropriately. Gradually extend the period between rewards for appropriate behaviour.

- If the child strips off her clothing, ensure that you put the child in overalls or other clothing that is difficult to remove.

- Ignore the stripping as much as possible—if necessary, stop the car and replace the child's clothes without any comment and without looking at the child.

Chapter 10
Managing Problem Behaviours at Preschool

- Aggression
- Destructive Behaviours
- Emptying out Toys
- Group Time
- Mealtimes
- Non-functional Play
- Painting
- Removing Clothing
- Rituals/ Obsessions
- Sand Play
- Screaming
- Sleep Time
- Social Isolation/ Wandering Alone
- Stealing Food
- Toileting
- Washing Hands/ Water Play

Aggression

Regular acts of aggression should not be ignored. The aggressor needs to understand that such behaviour is not acceptable, and an analysis of the behaviour should also be undertaken in order to determine why it is occurring (its function). Once we understand the functional message, we can intervene to modify the behaviour, either by teaching alternative communicative behaviours, teaching other functionally related alternative behaviours or intervening to modify the situation.

Intervention Strategies

- Whenever an act of aggression occurs, it is essential to look beyond the problem behaviour to the situation in which it occurs. Sometimes, we need to modify the situation as well as deal with the behaviour.

- Without commenting, push the child's hands down, give no eye contact and pay attention to the other child (the victim of the aggression).

- The behaviour may *not* continue if little fuss is made over it and the child does not receive the right reaction from people.

- If the behaviour continues to occur, then it cannot be ignored. However, you need to be aware that it may be the child's only way of interacting with other children. He may need, therefore, to be shown more appropriate ways to interact and play.

- Do not assume that the child knows what is acceptable behaviour and what is right or wrong. He may need to be taught that certain behaviours are not appropriate.

- One method of teaching a child that certain behaviours are not acceptable is to use a form of time out. As soon as the aggressive act occurs, remove the child from the situation by having him sit on the floor, a chair, carpet square or bean bag for 2–5 minutes. During this time, he is given no eye contact, no attention and no verbal reinforcements apart from, "No hitting/biting/ pinching" etc.

- Give attention to the other child. Ignore all tantrum behaviours, but as soon as the child is quiet or the 2–5 minutes have elapsed, divert him to another activity and give lots of attention and praise for behaving appropriately.

- Check closely the motivation for problem behaviour—if it is to avoid an unwanted situation, it is important to return the child to that situation, even if only for a short time. You do not want to encourage the child to use problem behaviours to avoid certain activities or situations.

- If you are aware of situations or activities that the child dislikes, look at ways of modifying them to become a more positive experience for the child—do not always force the child to comply with your terms.

- Time out is only effective if it is used *immediately* following the aggressive behaviour. The child will become confused if, while playing appropriately, he is put in time out for a behaviour that occurred some time ago—he then receives a mixed message that is very confusing.

- All staff should be involved in any behaviour-management program for aggression. They must all be firm and consistent so that the child is given a clear message.

For example, Billy is aggressive towards preschool staff, has severe tantrum behaviour and throws objects. These acts of aggression usually occur during structured teaching sessions.

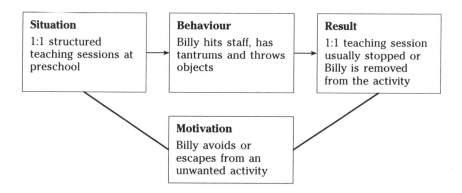

The functional message appears to be that Billy uses behaviour to escape activities that he does not understand or is not interested in. In this situation, it may be necessary to modify the situation in order to cater for Billy's particular needs.

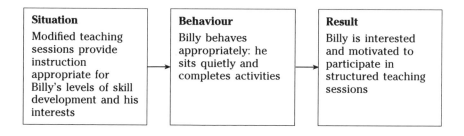

Initially, Billy should be assessed to determine his learning strengths and weaknesses and to ensure that any 1:1 program is meeting his needs in a positive way. The teaching sessions should then be modified to be more functional and instructional for Billy. The length of the teaching sessions may also need to be shortened initially and interspersed with brief breaks for Billy.

Destructive Behaviours

Children who engage in destructive behaviours at preschool are communicating a message to staff. The message may not be immediately obvious, but once a functional analysis of the behaviour is completed—which may involve collecting data over a period of time—some hypotheses about why the behaviour occurs can be formulated. It then becomes possible either to modify the situation or to teach the child alternative behaviours to assist him to cope in the preschool. These changes may include teaching additional communication and play skills and modifying the situation to include non-contingent reinforcement.

Intervention Strategies

- These behaviours produce very satisfying reactions from teachers and other children, and are very difficult to ignore.

- If these behaviours are allowed to continue unchecked, they will contribute to other children viewing the child with special needs as "different"; that is, as a child with a set of rules different from everyone else. All children should be made to feel that the efforts they make are respected and appreciated.

- The child should be shown appropriate ways to play with equipment, but you need to look beyond the behaviour in order to try to determine why it occurs.

- The child may enjoy the action of the objects falling when he destroys other children's constructions. He is probably unaware of the consequences of his actions and is unsympathetic towards other children's feelings—he is unaware of the chaos he is causing for the other children.

- The child may enjoy the reaction he receives from the staff and other children; he has to learn that it is not acceptable to destroy other children's work.

- Strategies may differ slightly depending on the situation. However, the important things to remember are to:

  give attention to the children who are the victims and assist them to make repairs;

  give no eye contact or attention to the child who has destroyed the work;

  quietly remove the offender from the situation.

- In some situations, such as block play, it may be appropriate to assist the child who has interfered with other children's work to make repairs to the destroyed work. It is important to ensure that the action does not become a game—when repairs are completed, the offending child should be redirected immediately to another activity.

- If the behaviour persists, a brief period in time out may be appropriate. In this case, as soon as the behaviour occurs, a stern "No!" followed by immediate removal to the time-out area might be effective. Ignore the child while he is in time out, and direct attention and assistance to the other child.

- A child who is looking for a reaction may tend to target more timid children or children who are more distressed by interference in their play. It may be helpful to encourage these children to be more assertive—tell them to say, "No!"

- If the child likes to watch the effect of toys falling, then he needs to be given his own equipment and assisted to build his own structures that he can then knock down.

- If the child has a favourite activity, toy or book that he can play with independently during times when he does not have 1:1 supervision, he should be encouraged to do this rather than wandering around destroying other children's work.

For example, Billy wanders around the preschool destroying other children's activities, especially during free-play sessions. Billy may spend 1 or 2 minutes at different activities, but then wanders away. He appears to lack direction, and just wanders around destroying things and then delighting in the chaos that follows.

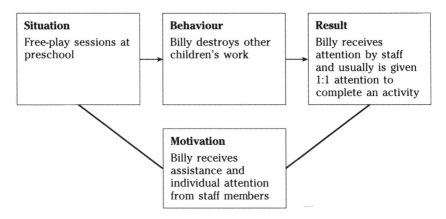

The message in this situation becomes quite clear after observation and data collection are completed, and the possible function of the behaviour is determined. Billy's problem behaviour is apparently being maintained by positive reinforcement from staff members, who offer immediate assistance and attention whenever Billy engages in destructive behaviour. The message being conveyed is that Billy wants attention and needs assistance to show him how to play independently.

On the basis of the analysis, Billy should to be taught additional skills, but the situation also needs to be modified to ensure that Billy receives positive reinforcement throughout the day.

Initially, an assessment to determine Billy's current play skills should be carried out and additional skills taught to enable him to play independently. Billy should also be taught some sharing and turn-taking skills to enable him to play with other children. Alternative means of communicating need for assistance should also be taught to Billy for times when he encounters a problem during independent work.

Second, the situation may be modified to provide Billy with reinforcement in the form of praise and attention at different times during the day when he is engaged in meaningful activities, either alone or with other children: Billy's free-play sessions may also initially be interspersed with short periods of 1:1 activity with a staff member.

Situation	Behaviour	Result
Free-play sessions are modified and Billy is taught additional communication and play skills	Billy plays more functionally and begins to share and take turns with other children	Billy is able to cope in free-play sessions and ask for assistance when required

Emptying out Toys

A child who wanders around the preschool classroom emptying out toys from boxes, sweeping equipment from shelves or watching objects fall from different heights obviously does not have appropriate play skills, or he enjoys the sensory stimulation of watching things fall.

A functional analysis of the child's behaviour over time will provide information to assist in determining exactly why the problem behaviour occurs. The child may need assistance in learning more meaningful play skills and developing alternative ways of obtaining sensory stimulation. The preschool may require same modification to ensure that toys and equipment are less accessible to the child.

Intervention Strategies

- Be aware of which toys and equipment are most often emptied out by the child—look closely and try to determine why certain things appeal more than others.
- Remove particular toys and equipment to a less accessible place.
- Emptying out toys or throwing toys onto the floor, off the table or over the shoulder may provide the child with some form of visual stimulation as he watches the toys fall. If this appears to be the case, restrict the number of toys available to the child at any one time and show him how to play with them appropriately.
- With certain toys, give the child only a few pieces in a separate box.
- Spend time teaching appropriate use with a limited number of pieces that must be picked up and returned to the box on completion of the activity.
- Place certain objects into containers with tight-fitting lids.
- With some activities, empty pieces out onto mat and remove the container—this removes the temptation for the child to empty out the pieces.
- Put out only enough equipment that is actually required for the activity.
- If shelves are on wheels or light enough, they may be turned around to face the wall when they are not in use to make equipment less accessible to the child.
- Put screens in front of shelves and put lids on containers. Once the child has learned not to empty out containers then it may be possible to leave equipment more visible.
- Praise child for appropriate behaviour—that is, for not emptying out containers.
- Keep the child occupied and stimulated—often problem behaviours occur when a child is left to wander and does not know how to occupy his time, and obtains enjoyment from the behaviour and the attention it brings.
- Constantly remind the child how to play appropriately with different equipment and toys.
- Ensure that the child is involved in packing away equipment, and praise him for helping.

- Teach the child to remove pieces one by one instead of tipping everything out at once, especially with puzzles, beads, Lego, blocks.

- Once the child empties out equipment, try to give minimal attention, but physically assist him to replace everything he has emptied out. Give no eye contact, make no fuss and merely give a verbal direction, "Pick up" or "Put in."

- Occasionally, depending on the situation, it may be simpler to ignore (if possible) the action—the child may eventually tire of the action if he receives no reinforcement.

- If the behaviour continues, you may need to try time out. As soon as the behaviour occurs, sit the child on a small chair or a beanbag. Give no eye contact or comment apart from a simple, "No".

For example, unless Billy is directed to a certain activity and assistance is given to show him how to complete the task, he tends to wander aimlessly around the room sweeping objects from shelves, emptying out boxes of toys and watching objects fall to the floor.

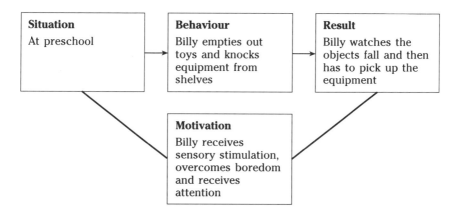

Situation	Behaviour	Result
At preschool	Billy empties out toys and knocks equipment from shelves	Billy watches the objects fall and then has to pick up the equipment

Motivation
Billy receives sensory stimulation, overcomes boredom and receives attention

After a functional analysis of the problem behaviour to determine why the behaviour occurs, a management program was implemented to show Billy that the particular behaviour was not acceptable. Billy was told to clean up the mess he made (minimal attention was given at this time), and assistance was given as necessary to ensure that he complied.

At the same time, Billy was taught other functionally related alternative behaviours, including more meaningful ways to use toys and equipment. It was acknowledged that Billy needed intermittent sensory respite that had been previously communicated through the problem behaviour, and so he was taught to play games that involved bouncing balls, filling and emptying water containers and helping to empty the rubbish bins. This allowed Billy to engage in sensory stimulation in a more appropriate way and under the control of preschool staff.

The situation was modified to ensure that Billy was reinforced for appropriate behaviour throughout the day so that attention was not contingent upon any problem behaviour.

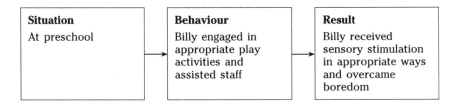

Situation	Behaviour	Result
At preschool	Billy engaged in appropriate play activities and assisted staff	Billy received sensory stimulation in appropriate ways and overcame boredom

Group Time

A child may not be able to sit quietly with the other children at group time, preferring either to withdraw to another part of the room or to cause a great deal of disruption. The child may not have the necessary skills to interact with other children, may not be able to remain attentive for any length of time or may not understand what is expected of him. For the child who has difficulty coping during group sessions, it may be necessary to modify the situation by simplifying the expectations upon the child, decreasing the number of demands upon the child and introducing individualised reinforcement. These changes are designed to provide a situation that places less pressure on the child.

Intervention Strategies

- Sit the child close to the teacher—in front of the teacher if possible and within arm's reach so that the teacher has control of the situation.
- If the child does not remain seated, have him sit on a small chair beside the group or beside the teacher—this may gradually be reduced to a small box, to a small piece of carpet or linoleum, but always close to the teacher or other adult. This helps the child to define his own space.
- If resources are available, have another adult sit with the child and remind him how to sit up straight with legs crossed— constantly reposition the child into a crosslegged position without comment.
- If the child continues to disturb and disrupt group time, move him to the edge of the main group and continue to physically assist him to sit correctly; give no eye contact.
- Don't get into a tug-of-war for control. If the situation becomes a battle, remove the child from the group entirely and have him help set out equipment, prepare morning tea or lay tables under the supervision of an assistant. Do not, however, offer the child a favourite or pleasant activity to complete—we do not want to reward his problem behaviour by allowing him to have a choice of toys.
- Reward the child for appropriate sitting—let him hold a favourite toy or give him a stamp; eventually aim to fade out rewards.
- Have a couple of maintenance activities available out of sight of the group—if the child becomes too restless or group time is too long, have one staff member withdraw the child to a quiet activity. Bring the child back to the group before the end of group time.

For example, Billy cries and has tantrums during group sessions. He refuses to sit with the other children and prefers to wander off to other parts of the room.

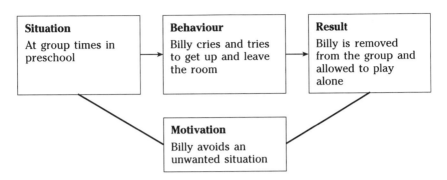

A functional analysis revealed that Billy's behaviour was rein-forced when staff allowed him to leave or avoid unwanted situa-tions. The message from Billy was, "I don't want to do this/I don't understand and I want to leave." The staff looked closely at the group session to determine why Billy wanted to avoid the situation. It was hypothesised that Billy, because of delayed communication and social skills, did not understand what was happening and was also unable to concentrate for too long.

Initially, Billy was taught alternative communicative means of indicating his desire to escape. He was taught the manual sign to leave, and was encouraged to use it in certain situations. The situ-ation was also modified and staff expectations of Billy were also lowered. Billy was expected to remain with the group for a few minutes at the start of the group session and then return to the group toward the end of the session. At other times, Billy was allowed to leave the group to complete other activities with an assistant. These included assisting to set up tables for lunch, read-ing stories or listening to tapes. Billy was reinforced for sitting and listening. Over time, Billy's time with the group was gradually extended.

Mealtimes

Mealtimes at preschool can be stressful if a child displays inappropriate behaviour while other children are sitting quietly, eating and socially interacting with each other. Mealtimes are social times of the day, but occasionally, a child may not have developed any functional social skills. He steals other children's food, throws food and drink and refuses to sit with the other children. Another child may have no interest in food or eating, and so is not motivated to sit at the table and eat morning tea or lunch. This child constantly gets out of his seat, refuses to eat and will have tantrums and scream if forced to sit at the table for the whole mealtime.

Intervention Strategies

- Have the child seated in a regular place at a table with children who are not likely to allow him to steal food from them.
- Seat the child close to the teacher or assistant.
- Have the adult sit behind the child so as to be within reach of the child's hands. If the child attempts to stand up or lunge forward to steal food, gently put him back on his chair.
- Reward the child for "good sitting".

- If the child attempts to steal food, move his chair out from the table so that he can only reach his own food. Pull his arms back to his own food and give no eye contact. Comment on appropriate behaviour.

- If the child is a messy eater, allow the adult to keep control of the lunchbox, and hand over small amounts of food to the child in correct sequence (sandwiches, biscuits, fruit, drink).

- If the child finishes eating before the other children and is unable to sit quietly and wait for others to finish, allow the child to leave the table and move on to another activity. Gradually extend his time sitting until he is able to stay with the group until the end of the lunch period.

- Allow the child to choose a favourite book or toy to play with quietly on a mat after lunch until the other children are all finished and ready to move on to the next activity.

- If the child gets out of his chair and attempts to wander around the room while still eating, take the food away from him and put it back on the table. Bring the child back to the table and remind him, "*No sitting, no food.*"

- The child may require close supervision with drinks and occasional physical prompts to "hold cup" correctly. To begin with, pour only small amounts of liquid into the cup, especially if the child throws things or tips things out (less mess to clean up). Gradually, add more liquid to the cup and withdraw the physical assistance.

- If the child refuses to eat at preschool, make sure that the food provided is similar to what the child normally eats at home— not what the parents think that he should eat or what they want staff to force him to eat.

- Do not attempt to force the child to eat, simply place the food on the table in front of the child; eventually, if he is hungry enough (and not able to steal food from another child), he will begin to eat. Some children take weeks or even months to settle down and become confident at preschool, and so may not eat much until that time. Understand the child's fears and do not force him to conform totally. At first, merely concentrate on having the child sit at the table for short periods.

- If a child refuses to eat with the group, he may feel more comfortable away from the other children. Try putting the child at a table away from the group and gradually reducing the distance, without distressing the child, until he is back with the other children.

For example, Billy is most disruptive at mealtimes. He refuses to sit at the table with the other children, cries and has tantrums, throws food and drink and refuses to eat lunch.

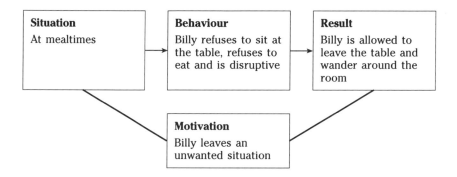

After studying Billy's behaviour, it was felt that there were a number of issues that needed to be addressed if Billy was to learn to cope at mealtimes. The message was obvious that Billy did not want to remain at the table during mealtimes, but it was not so obvious why this was the case.

The issues addressed by staff to increase Billy's interest and comfort at mealtimes included teaching Billy some new skills (sitting, tolerating other people in close proximity, alternative ways to communicate anxiety and stress) and also trying to increase Billy's interest in food by offering small portions of different food, but not forcing him to eat.

The mealtime was also modified for Billy, and he was allowed to sit at a table away from the other children (other children were gradually introduced to his table), the time he was expected to remain seated was shortened and he was allowed to leave the table for another activity after a certain time.

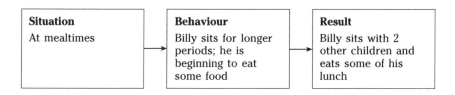

See also "Stealing Food".

Non-functional Play

When some young children start at preschool, they are unable to engage in appropriate play with other children. Some children may not yet have developed play skills, having had little opportunity to play with other children at home; some children are withdrawn and not interested in interacting or playing with toys; and other children may have established non-functional play behaviours and rituals that need to be modified.

Functional play skills include knowing how to imitate, share with others, take turns, engage in pretend play and relate to others in a meaningful way.

Before any intervention program can be considered, a functional analysis should be undertaken in order to understand why the behaviour is occurring. This analysis should be completed in the situation where the behaviour occurs—the preschool.

For example, since starting preschool, Mary has stood out as being different. She prefers to withdraw from the other children, and often seems unaware or uninterested in what is happening around her. She has no idea about sharing or taking turns, and will destroy other children's work; she fixates on certain objects and will spend long periods of time lining up toys, sifting sand through her fingers, playing with water in the bathroom sink or flicking through the pages of a book.

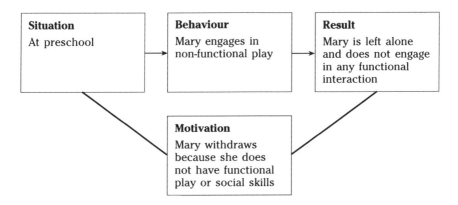

Mary's behaviours keep her isolated from the other children and prevent her from learning any functional play or social skills. A functional analysis allowed staff to hypothesise that Mary did not know how the play appropriately, she enjoyed the sensory feedback from some of her repetitive activities and she lacked awareness of other people's needs.

In order to facilitate Mary's full integration into the preschool program, a number of intervention strategies were established. Initially, some of the preschool sessions were modified to ensure that Mary was given the opportunity to play and interact with other children in small groups (one or two other children). Structured play sessions were introduced for Mary and activities were included that involved alternative ways of playing with toys, turn-taking, sharing and pretend play. Mary was socially reinforced through praise and hugs for completing activities, and her work was labelled (as was the work of other children) and Mary was encouraged to take pride in her work and to accept social interaction.

Times were allocated during the day so that Mary had opportunities to engage in sensory stimulation, but the activities were more structured (for example, sand play—Mary was encouraged to fill and empty containers, dig holes and build castles; water play—Mary was encouraged to fill containers and then pour out the water, to paint with water and to bath the dolls).

Mary was monitored when she went to the bathroom, discouraged from playing in the sink and taught how to wash her hands properly.

Finally, Mary was encouraged to communicate verbally and non-verbally to indicate her wants and needs.

Situation		Behaviour		Result
At preschool	→	Mary engages in appropriate play and is beginning to socialise with other children	→	Mary's skills have improved and she does not stand out as different from other children

See also "Painting", "Sand Play" and "Washing Hands/Water Play".

Painting

Some young children, on first entering preschool, do not have age-appropriate play skills. They are unable to follow the normal routines and rules of the preschool, and do not seem to be aware of or understand the feelings of the other children. They will usually exhibit inappropriate, problem behaviours during structured and unstructured play activities. During painting sessions, they may destroy other children's work, attempt to paint at someone else's easel, take other children's paint and brushes or actively try to avoid participating.

Intervention Strategies

- The child may initially require physical prompting throughout the painting activity—when he is learning to paint at an easel, he may forget which is his painting.

- Stand behind the child when he is painting, and if he moves to go around the other side of the easel, say nothing, give no eye contact, but physically bring the child's hand and brush back to his own paper.

- When the child is painting, give positive feedback about his painting efforts and the fact that he is using his own paper and easel.

- Make a big fuss over the finished product—"All finished, great painting." Assist the child to hang the painting to dry. Emphasis should be placed upon the beginning and end of the activity.

- Explain to other children that the child is only learning to paint and may need to be reminded about where to paint.

- If the child enjoys painting, allow him to repeat the activity as long as he attempts some other activities as well.

- A child may dislike painting because he does not like the tactile sensation of touching messy paint. Take the child's hand as he passes the easels, gently place a brush in his hands and assist him to complete one stroke on the paper. Move on immediately to other activities, but return to the painting corner and repeat the action several times during the session.

- Gradually increase the amount of time that the child spends at the easel painting, and praise the child for attempting the activity.

- If a child loves painting but destroys other children's work, as soon as he has completed his painting, move him on to another activity away from the painting corner to lessen the temptation to return to the activity.

See also "Non-functional Play".

Removing Clothing

The child who continually strips off his clothing and runs around naked is displaying a problem behaviour that needs to be discouraged. It is not a behaviour that can be ignored. He may strip off clothing because he does not like the feel of fabric against his skin, he may prefer the freedom of being naked, he may not feel the cold or he may like the reaction and attention he receives from preschool staff and other children whenever he strips.

Intervention Strategies

- Suggest to parents that they dress the child in clothing that is difficult to remove—overalls, playsuits with zips at the back, pants with loops and a belt that the child can't undo, skivvies in winter, T-shirts or sweaters with buttons at the neck or shirts with small buttons.
- Try to divert the child at the first sign of stripping. Without comment, lead the child to an activity and help him to participate.
- If clothing is removed, assist the child to dress again quickly and without smiling, commenting or giving eye contact.
- Find activities that the child can complete without being able to get at his clothing—for example, play a game of rolling up and unrolling in a blanket, circle games where children hold hands.
- Do not chase the child to dress him—it gives too much attention and becomes a game. Ignore the child until you can calmly apprehend him and assist him to dress.
- Use tactile games with the child in order to desensitise his skin. Use rough towels to rub over body, use silk, satin, wool, cotton, etc. and encourage the child to touch them.

- Play peek-a-boo with different textured scarves.
- Encourage the child to play with play dough, shaving cream, finger painting, etc., for tactile experiences.
- Sometimes in hot weather, the children may be allowed to strip off and run around under the sprinkler in a wading pool. This may be confusing for the child, but he has to learn that stripping may be appropriate in some circumstances, but not at other times.

For example, Billy strips off his clothing at preschool, preferring to run around naked. Billy does not appear to feel changes in temperature, and he cries and has tantrums when forced to wear too much clothing. At home, Billy refuses to get dressed and becomes extremely agitated if forced to wear clothing.

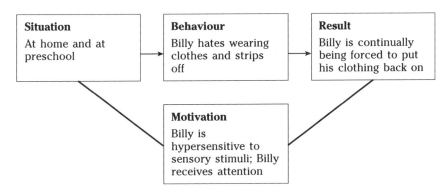

It was hypothesised that Billy disliked wearing clothes because he was uncomfortable with the feeling of different fabrics against his skin. The behaviour was reinforced by the attention Billy received when he stripped.

In order to decrease the problem behaviour, Billy was taught other functionally related alternative responses, and the situation was modified to provide more non-contingent reinforcement to Billy.

Some strategies were implemented to desensitise Billy to tactile hypersensitivity. Tactile experiences were introduced throughout the day (tickle games, touch games, finger painting, etc.). Initially, Billy was allowed to wear only training pants during the day. Additional clothing was gradually introduced (a T-shirt with a favourite cartoon character on the front) until Billy was able to tolerate wearing shorts and a T-shirt.

A rule was introduced at both home and preschool that Billy was not allowed to play outdoors unless he was wearing his shoes. As Billy loved to go out, this was a powerful motivator.

At home and at preschool, when Billy stripped off his clothing, he was immediately told, "Pants on", and handed his training pants. Physical assistance was given as necessary, but eye contact and attention was kept to a minimum. Everyone was careful about positively reinforcing Billy throughout the day when he was wearing some clothing.

Situation	Behaviour	Result
At home and at preschool	Billy wears his training pants and T-shirt	Billy is reinforced throughout the day for appropriate behaviour and spends less time stripping

Rituals/Obsessions

A child may spend his time at preschool isolated from other children, rigidly following some clearly defined rituals or obsessively lining up objects, playing only with certain toys and repeating set questions over and over. The child uses these rituals and obsessions to help him to cope in unfamiliar situations and to bring him some sense of control over his environment.

Unfortunately, the rituals and obsessions interfere with the child's opportunities to learn and experience new activities. The child's reliance on rituals and obsessions restrict his chances to improve his skills and to socialise and play with other children. Most obsessive children have very poorly developed play skills, and do not know how to engage in pretend or creative play.

Once we understand the function behind the problem behaviour, we can begin to teach the child alternative play skills, encourage communication skills and improve the child's confidence to cope in new situations. The key is to provide the child with alternative, functional ways to use objects and skills to interact with people.

Intervention Strategies

- Be aware of the child who appears to be happily playing with the same piece of equipment over and over again in a repetitive way. For example,

    building blocks in lines, lining up cars;

    flicking through books, not stopping to look at the pictures;

    playing with cars or trains, lying on the floor and pushing them back and forth in front of his eyes;

    sitting in the sandpit sifting sand through his fingers;

    wandering around the room, stopping briefly at activities and then continuing to the next one without completing any;

    tipping equipment out, watching it fall to the ground and then wandering off.

- For all of the above, encourage the child to complete what he has started in a more meaningful way, even if physical prompts are necessary. The aim is to show the child alternative ways to play and receive enjoyment from the activity.

- All staff must work together to decide what the child should accomplish—choose a few activities and work with the child on these until he masters them; for example, physically help the child to paint with all colours and put the brushes back where they belong. Make a fuss over the finished painting and ignore any tantrum behaviour.

- Some children find all activities confusing and see little point in doing them—they may not know how to use the equipment and must be shown again and again because they may lack imaginative or creative play skills.

- If the child appears confused and not sure of what is expected of him, he may require some physical assistance until he understands what to do.
- Sit with the child and model more constructive play—for example, build a simple bridge and a block train and then push the train under the bridge.
- Change the activity to stacking blocks, take turns with the child to put a block on, possibly including a second child in the activity.
- If the child becomes distressed at you interfering with his obsession, it may be best to pack the toys away with his assistance and redirect the child to something else, preferably something quite different.
- Almost anything can be lined up—crayons, play dough, cars, etc. With all objects, try to show the child a more constructive way to play, either by encouraging him to imitate your behaviour or by placing your hands over the child's to guide them to more appropriate play.
- If the lining up or other obsessive behaviour persists and begins to interfere with the child's participation in different activities, then change the activity and redirect the child away from certain objects.
- Always reinforce appropriate play with praise.
- A child's obsessions may be used as a reward for the child once he has completed a teacher-directed activity. This use of obsessions should be allowed only under the teacher's control and for a specified period of time (for example, 5 minutes).
- If the child obsessively plays with a certain toy in the same way, model additional ways to play with the toy and encourage the child to participate. Gradually bring in other toys and other children to play with the child.
- If the child insists on following certain rituals, it may be necessary to gradually change these by restricting the steps in the ritual, the number of objects involved or the amount of time the child needs to complete the ritual.

For example, Billy spent most of his time at preschool following rituals and engaging in obsessive play. Billy had to touch all of the chairs in the room before he would sit down; he would smell all food before eating it and he would line up all the pieces of equipment before he would complete an activity. Billy enjoyed the block corner where he would line up all the blocks according to size and sort all of the building bricks according to colour. Billy became agitated if any of his rituals or obsessions were interfered with.

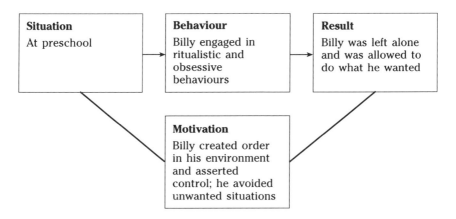

Once a functional analysis was completed, a number of hypotheses were formulated to explain why Billy engaged in the problem behaviours. It was felt that Billy used rituals and obsessions to assert control over his environment and to bring order to unfamiliar situations. Billy was not able to function appropriately at preschool because he did not have the necessary skills. A program was implemented to teach Billy some basic communication, social and play skills, and he was encouraged to use these skills at preschool to enhance his enjoyment and participation in the daily preschool programs. Gradually, his need for rituals and obsessions decreased as he became more comfortable with the normal preschool routines.

As Billy seemed to function best in a structured setting, time was spent teaching Billy the routines of the program and ensuring that *all* staff and children followed these. Over time, these routines were occasionally modified in order to teach Billy to tolerate and cope with changes in his routine and new situations.

Sand Play

Non-functional sand play may include obsessive behaviour such as sifting sand through the fingers, throwing sand in an attempt to avoid an unwanted situation or for sensory stimulation, destroying

other children's creations, and refusing to attempt any activities in the sandpit. The child who sits quietly in the sand and lets it drizzle through his fingers may be exploring the texture or be visually stimulated by the falling sand particles. The sifting behaviour may also be obsessive, and the child may need to do this at times in order to relax and block out a surrounding environment that at times may appear overwhelming and strange.

Non-functional play may also occur because the child does not know how to play more appropriately with other children or even alone in the sandpit. Some children lack creative or imaginative play and need to be shown how to play.

Intervention Strategies

- Decide on an activity that you would like the child to accomplish (for example, fill a bucket with sand using a spade, turn it upside down to make a castle and then encourage the child to push it over).

- Sit behind the child (or beside or in front of him), hold his hand on the spade and assist him to dig and fill the bucket. Encourage the child to complete the activity, withdrawing assistance as the child becomes more actively involved.

- Show the child how to play with toys such as trucks and cars in the sandpit, especially if he pushes them appropriately when he is inside. Some children have trouble generalising skills across different situations and may need to be shown how to play with equipment in each situation.
- Provide sand toys that are easy to manoeuvre—small buckets and spades, cars, etc.
- Sit with the child and model appropriate sand play—push a car, fill a bucket, etc.
- Praise the child for appropriate play—for example, "That's good digging" (depending on the action).
- When the child tires of the activity or if you have to move on to something else, it may be best to redirect the child to another area so that he does not go back to his non-functional play.
- Ensure that the child does not remain in the sandpit for the entire outdoor period.
- Draw the child's attention to the other children playing in the sand: "Look at Mary digging." Try to include another child in the activity: "Mary, you help Billy to dig."
- Encourage the other children to involve the child in meaningful play in different situations. Other children are by far the best and most appropriate role models for children who do not know how to play appropriately.
- Once the child has developed some appropriate play skills in the sandpit such as digging, making sandcastles, building road-ways for toy cars and filling buckets with sand, then introduce another child into the activity, and encourage them to play together and share the toys.
- If the child begins to throw the sand or interfere inappropriately in other children's play activities, it may be necessary to redirect the child to another activity and assist him to complete that activity, before returning him to the sandpit and showing him some ways to play.

See also "Non-functional Play".

Screaming

The child who screams continually is using this problem behaviour to convey a message. The behaviour is not uncommon among children with delayed communication skills—children who are unable to express themselves verbally. Screaming is an attempt to

communicate when the child does not have the appropriate skills to vocalise his needs and desires. A lack of functional communication can be very frustrating for the child, leading to an increase in problem behaviour as the child increasingly tries to find ways to communicate.

Generally, the reason for screaming behaviour is to communicate needs and desires. A breakdown of the behaviour in order to understand specific messages will require a study of the behaviour in *context*. The child may be attempting to gain attention and the message may be: "Pay attention to me"; the child may be attempting to avoid an unwanted situation and the message may be: "I don't want to do this anymore"; the child may be asking for help; telling you that he is bored, anxious or hurt; or the message may be that the child does not understand what is expected of him.

Any management program for inappropriate screaming would therefore involve providing the child with alternative ways of communicating, as well as looking closely at situational factors that may be influencing the behaviour.

Intervention Strategies

- Most problem behaviours occur for a reason. When a child continually screams, it is important to look beyond the screaming to what was occurring immediately before in order to understand the function of the behaviour.

- The child may scream in order to gain attention—the other children and the staff usually look and react when a child screams. Attention should be given to the child during the day so that it is not contingent on the screaming behaviour.

- The child may scream to avoid a certain situation—for example, he does not want to complete an activity, he does not want another child sitting near him, he does not want to share his toys. Look closely at the situation to find out why the child is not able to cope.

- The child may scream as a form of communication when he does not have the appropriate skills to vocalise correctly. The child needs to be shown alternative, functional ways to communicate—signing, gesturing, pointing to pictures.

- In the preschool, it is very difficult to ignore the screaming and not react, because all the children turn and look. If it is attention-seeking behaviour, try to ignore it. If necessary, move the other children away from the child and go on with what you were doing. Attention should be given to the child when he is attempting to communicate in other ways.

- Remove the "screamer" from the situation, give no eye contact or comments, *but* be sure to reward the child for quiet behaviour—lots of positive attention, smiles, tickles or verbal comments.

- If the child appears to use screaming as a way of avoiding an unwanted or unfamiliar situation, it may be necessary to change the situation a little to accommodate the child's fears/needs. At the same time, the child has to learn that the problem behaviour will not be successful in allowing him to avoid a situation. Even if the child is screaming, he should be assisted if necessary to at least partially complete the activity.

- If the child screams to avoid sitting with the other children at group time, modify the situation, bring him to sit with the group at the last possible moment. Gradually increase the time that he remains seated with the group. Let him move away from the group only at a time when he is quiet, and encourage him to come back to the group toward the end of the group session so that he is seated at the end of the activity.

- The child may be excited by the amount of stimulation and activity around him. Try to find a quiet, calm activity, such as looking at a book, doing a puzzle, playing with water. Ignore as much screaming as possible—no comments, no eye contact. Persevere with the activities and reinforce any quiet play with praise, smiles and touch if the child enjoys this.

- If screaming behaviour persists or increases despite all efforts to modify it, and after consistently ignoring it for at least a couple of weeks, you may need to try time out. This should be implemented as soon as the behaviour occurs. At the same time, attempts should continue to provide the child with alternative ways of communicating.

For example, Billy had a high-pitched scream that he used at preschool whenever people tried to interact with him in any way. Billy threw himself to the floor and screamed until he was left alone to play by himself. Billy's screaming was extremely upsetting for the other children and disruptive to the preschool program.

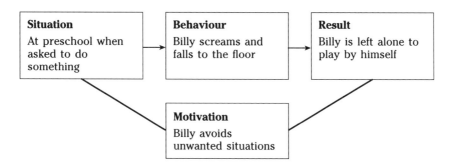

Situation	Behaviour	Result
At preschool when asked to do something	Billy screams and falls to the floor	Billy is left alone to play by himself

Motivation
Billy avoids unwanted situations

A functional analysis of Billy's behaviour revealed that his attempts to avoid interactive situations were because he did not fully understand what was expected of him, and he did not have the skills to interact socially with other people.

An intervention strategy was designed to teach Billy alternative communicative behaviour, and extensive modelling was introduced to show Billy ways of interacting with others. The staff looked closely at how they were communicating with Billy, and realised the need to simplify their communication by using visual cues to assist Billy to understand, and, when necessary, to physically assist him to complete activities. Activities were introduced to develop Billy's receptive language skills so that he was more able to understand verbal language.

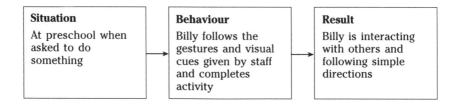

Situation	Behaviour	Result
At preschool when asked to do something	Billy follows the gestures and visual cues given by staff and completes activity	Billy is interacting with others and following simple directions

Sleep Time

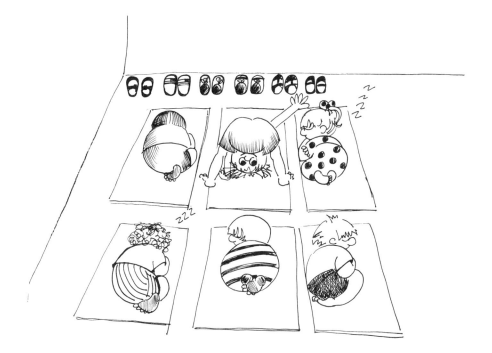

Sleep time at preschool may be a difficult time for children who are not good sleepers or who find it difficult remaining quiet and still for too long.

If a child refuses to sleep or to remain on his bed during sleep time, he may engage in some problem behaviours that disrupt the other children. If this occurs, it may be preferable to remove the child from the situation until his behaviour improves, and then gradually bring him back to the main group when he is less disruptive. Some children need to learn the routine of the preschool centre and to understand the rules, especially if they are not used to having an afternoon sleep at home.

Intervention Strategies

- Remember that some children do not normally sleep in the afternoon and may need time to get used to the idea of having a nap.
- If child is not a "sleeper", it may be necessary to shorten the expected sleep time initially and gradually increase the time spent remaining on the bed.

- With some children, it may be necessary to change the period from sleep time to quiet time. You cannot force a child to sleep, you can only make the environment conducive to sleeping by dimming lights, playing soft music and keeping all distractions to a minimum.
- If the child remains disruptive, remove his bed away from other children; screen it off, if possible. This limits usual feedback. Gradually move the child back to the group as his resting behaviour improves.
- Provide adult supervision to settle the child and encourage him to remain on his bed.
- The adult supervisor should:

    pat the child only if he is lying down;

    constantly reposition the child to lie down;

    give no eye contact or attention verbally.
- Offer the child a book or a soft toy to look at when he is lying down. As soon as the child sits up, remove the book. Lie the child back down and return the book. As the child completes a book, exchange it for another. Recycle books throughout rest time. The emphasis remains on having the child lie down quietly during the rest period. Eventually, the child may fall asleep.
- Check with parents to see if the child has special objects (such as a soft toy or a special pillow) he needs at home at sleep time—this could be brought to preschool to help the child feel comfortable and relaxed.
- If a child does not like to be touched, do not pat him off to sleep; merely sit beside him quietly so that he is aware of your presence.
- If the child gets up, physically put him back to bed with *no* eye contact and *no* comment.
- If the child has tantrums at rest time, it is best to remove him to another room until he has learned to remain quietly on his bed; this may take some time and 1:1 supervision.
- Start with short periods of time and reward the child for remaining on his bed. You may need to break up the sleep period—take the child outside for a walk or to another room to complete a quiet activity, and then return the child to bed before the end of sleep period. Gradually increase the time spent on the bed as the child becomes more compliant. Increase the period on the bed at both ends of rest period, that is, leave him on the bed longer before engaging in an activity and bring him back to bed earlier.

- If possible, let the child be the last to lie down to rest, and praise the child for getting onto the bed quietly.

For example, when Billy first started preschool, he refused to remain on his bed at sleep time. He continually jumped up, climbed over other children and squealed and babbled loudly.

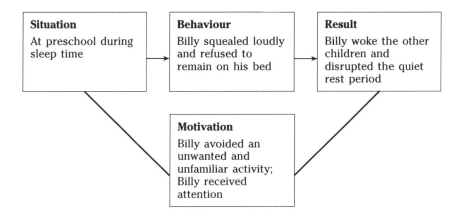

Billy did not normally have an afternoon sleep at home and did not understand the routine at preschool. He preferred to remain active and could not understand why he was not allowed to run around and play. Billy's behaviour indicated that he did not understand what he was expected to do at sleep time and was not used to quiet afternoon activities.

Billy was initially removed from the main group and allowed to complete several quiet activities with a staff member during the sleep period. These included reading stories, completing puzzles and drawing pictures. He was expected to remain on his bed for short periods and allowed to sit at a table for the remainder of the time. The time spent on his bed was gradually extended. No attempts were made to force Billy to lie down—he was allowed to sit on his bed and play as long as he remained quiet. Social reinforcement was given to Billy for quietly sitting, and attention was minimised whenever he was disruptive.

Once Billy was able to remain on his bed for a designated time period (perhaps 20 minutes), his bed was moved back to the group and he was encouraged to lie down and rest (the atmosphere was set with dimmed light, soft music, no distraction and a favourite toy to hold). If Billy was unable to remain quiet for the entire sleep period, he was allowed to get up after a certain time and play quietly by himself.

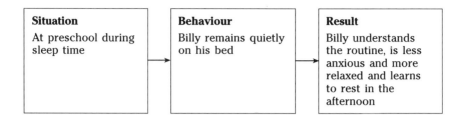

Situation	Behaviour	Result
At preschool during sleep time	Billy remains quietly on his bed	Billy understands the routine, is less anxious and more relaxed and learns to rest in the afternoon

Social Isolation/Wandering Alone

Occasionally, a child enters preschool with severely delayed social and communication skills. The child may be unable to communicate verbally, and will often use inappropriate behaviour to indicate his wants and needs. The child may also appear aloof and withdrawn—unable and unwilling to play with the other children. This child does not have the skills to relate to others verbally and non-verbally and, just as important, does not appear to have any desire to do so.

A functional analysis of the behaviour of a child who isolates himself from others usually indicates the need to teach the child new, functional behaviours that will lead to reinforcing consequences, similar to those that the child receives from the problem behaviour. The child who voluntarily isolates himself from others maintains control over his environment—he does not allow any new experiences to impinge on him, and therefore does not have to cope with any unfamiliar and unwanted situations.

The child needs to be taught how to relate to others, and the situation should be structured to such an extent that the desire to relate is also encouraged. The child may also need to be taught some basic play skills. This may be a long-term goal taking months or even years to achieve fully.

There are many ways to encourage a child to become more involved in the general routines and activities of the preschool, and some possible intervention strategies are listed below.

Intervention Strategies

- Many preschool centres have a period of free play following busy morning activities. At this time, some children may need "down time" to unwind following the demands of participating in indoor activities and simply being inside with so many other children— allow the children time to wind down before encouraging further interaction.

- Allow the child some free time to be alone and wander if he pleases.

- After 5–10 minutes, go to the child and lead him to an activity— for example, water play or sand play—and show him how to participate appropriately.

- Praise the child for participating, and draw his attention to other children playing at the same activity.

- Five minutes may be long enough initially (for some children it may be too long) to actively engage the child in a task before leaving him to choose where he wants to play.

- If the child returns to isolated wandering around the perimeter, leave him for 5–10 minutes and then repeat the procedure with a different activity.

- It is OK to let the child wander off at times, but he needs to be encouraged to join in with activities and normal preschool routines.

- Look at why the child may be isolated and wandering alone. It could be because he is unsure of how to use the equipment or he lacks play skills and is not sure how to initiate play; perhaps he just does not want to join in and prefers to be alone—some skills may need to be taught to the child using imitation, modelling, exploration.

- At group times, it is important that the child participates at least partially. He should be encouraged to join in and be part of the group at the beginning of the session. When he becomes anxious or fidgety, allow him to wander off or remove him from the group, but bring him back before the end of the session. Gradually increase the amount of time that the child is expected to remain with the group.

- Bring the child into small groups of children playing in order to show him how to play appropriately and use the equipment— use other children as role models. Eventually, the child's behaviour may develop from solitary to parallel.

- Increase the child's awareness of other children by encouraging small-group activities. Introduce turn-taking games. Initially, play 1:1 with the child taking turns—for example, building a tower, putting pegs in a board, filling a bucket with sand—and when this is mastered, bring in another child and increase the numbers until the child is part of a small group.

- If the child has tantrums when he is brought into an activity, persevere—it may be because he doesn't like being directed or he doesn't understand what is expected of him. It is important to insist that the child finishes the activity, as you do not want the child thinking that if he screams and has tantrums he can avoid the situation.

- Gradually, as the child becomes more familiar with his surroundings and the routines of the preschool, the wandering and isolation may decrease.

No child should have to be meaningfully occupied every minute of the day.

For example, when Billy started preschool, he showed no interest in the routines and play activities, and appeared unaware of the other children. Billy was more interested in certain objects, and preferred to spend most of the day wandering around the perimeters of the outdoor play area looking at the straight lines created by the fence posts.

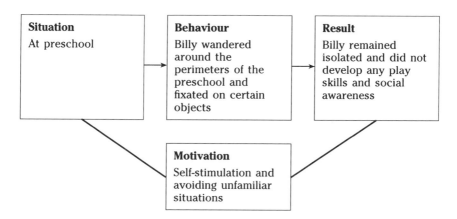

A functional analysis indicated that Billy's self-isolation seemed to be related to his inability to socialise and to play. Billy seemed to exhibit the behaviour to stimulate himself because he was not able to be stimulated through external variables. The behaviour was interpreted to mean, "I'm not getting the input I want and I'm bored" and also, "I'm overwhelmed and I don't know how to cope."

It was decided to provide direct instruction to teach Billy alternative appropriate behaviours that would give him more functional ways to be stimulated and develop skills to allow him to cope in the group situation. Direct teaching methods were used to show Billy how to play with the toys and equipment at preschool. Initially, these teaching sessions were kept short and Billy was allowed to wander between sessions. Gradually, another child was introduced into the teaching sessions and activities were modified to include turn-taking and imitation.

Billy was encouraged to participate in group activities throughout the day but was also allowed to wander off when he had had enough.

Billy's new play skills were generalised to different settings in the preschool, and Billy was encouraged to be involved in a number of different activities, including water play, painting, dressing-up, sand play, block corner and chasing games. These activities all involved working closely with other children.

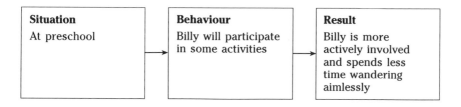

Stealing Food

If a child is not used to having set mealtimes at home, he may initially have difficulty adapting to the routine of the preschool. Some children prefer to eat small amounts of food throughout the day rather than sit down for set meals. If food is not always available, they may go looking for it, and steal it from other children's lunchboxes or wherever they find it. A child may be bored and go looking for food, while someone else may be obsessed with food or eating and be unable to discriminate among foods. Another child may simply prefer what another child has for lunch.

- Ensure that all food is stored in a secure place away from the child in order to lessen the temptation.
- As part of the morning routine on arrival at preschool, have all children sort their food into separate morning tea and lunch baskets. This ensures that no food is left in bags that are easily accessible. The baskets should be kept out of sight until required.
- A stressed or bored child is more likely to be tempted to steal food than a child who is kept busy and stimulated.
- Establish a set routine for mealtimes that is easily followed. If a child attempts to steal food or demands food at inappropriate times, simply remind him that it will be morning tea/lunchtime after outside play/group time or whatever activity usually occurs.

- If a child is caught eating from someone's lunchbox, simply remove the food, say, "No stealing", and return the child to the previous activity; remove the food from the child's reach.
- If you suspect that the child may be hungry or may have missed breakfast, offer a small piece of fruit, but insist that the child sits at the table to eat.
- Stealing food may be the child's attempt to gain attention. Ensure that the child is given lots of praise and attention for appropriate behaviour, and remove the temptation to steal food by placing lunchboxes out of reach.

See also "Mealtimes".

Toileting

Toileting skills or lack of toileting skills should not be seen as a problem behaviour, but rather as skills not yet learned. Children develop toileting skills at different ages, and some children may have difficulty generalising this skill from one environment to another.

A child who refuses to sit on the toilet at preschool even though he uses the toilet appropriately at home may be presenting with a problem behaviour. Looking at the behaviour in context will help to determine the particular message that the child is attempting to convey. The child who refuses to use the preschool toilet and who holds on all day until he gets home is communicating that he is anxious and unsure, especially of the new setting and the new routines. Some children require structure and familiarity in order to cope, and have great difficulty in dealing with changes in their lives.

Another problem behaviour related to toileting that occasionally manifests itself at preschool concerns the child who deliberately soils himself in order to avoid unwanted situations or to gain attention.

Some intervention strategies to help with toileting problems at preschool follow. It is essential when faced with such a problem behaviour to look at it in the context in which it occurs in order to determine the function of the behaviour, rather than merely to try some different strategies that may or may not work.

Intervention Strategies

- Don't pressure the child or make a fuss when accidents occur.
- The first aim is to have the child sit on the toilet without fear or anger.
- Once the child is happy to sit on the toilet, then it is time to start taking him regularly and training him to use the toilet.
- The child also needs to be trained to pull his pants down, sit independently, wipe himself, pull pants up, flush the toilet and wash his hands.
- Initially, take the child to the toilet during routine times at preschool (approximately every hour or at certain times during the day).
- Give physical assistance to:

  pull pants down; sit on the toilet; pull pants up; press button to flush toilet; turn the tap on; wash hands; turn the tap off; dry hands.

  NB: if the child is still wearing nappies, remove the nappy and sit the child on the toilet for a minute before replacing a clean nappy.

- If the child refuses to sit on the toilet, try to physically hold him there for a few seconds to begin with and gradually extend the time. Keep his attention with a favourite toy, bubbles, tickles, etc.
- If the child does not urinate, do not make a fuss or comment. Reward him for sitting on the toilet. Build up from there.
- Slowly decrease the physical assistance until he can complete the toileting with verbal reminders.

- If the child uses the toilet, immediately reward him with praise, cuddles, etc.
- A child may feel threatened by the unfamiliar bathroom and routine when he first starts preschool. Encourage the child to enter the bathroom at different routine times, but do not pressure the child to use the toilet. Have him wash his hands before leaving the bathroom so that he starts to understand the toileting routine. Eventually, encourage the child to sit on the toilet (pants up, flush toilet, wash hands) before leaving the bathroom. Understand the child's anxiety and remain very positive with him.
- A child may soil himself to avoid an activity or for attention. Look at why the child is using this behaviour to avoid a situation, and *modify* the situation. Give the child reinforcement throughout the day so that attention is not contingent upon the problem behaviour.

Washing Hands/Water Play

Most children love to play with water—especially the taps in the bathroom. Some children do not realise the consequences of their actions, but experience obvious enjoyment from just watching the water.

Intervention Strategies

- Water is both soothing and exciting, and the bored child will love the stimulation he receives from playing with water.
- Ensure maximum supervision of the child who plays with the bathroom taps. If the child enters the bathroom, remove him immediately with, "Let's wait for wash-hands time." Allow the child into the bathroom area only during routine times when staff are supervising.
- If the child escapes to the bathroom and is playing at the sink, place the child's hands on the taps and say, "1, 2, 3, tap off", rather than saying something negative. This routine should also be followed at normal wash times so the child learns to expect water to run from the taps for a brief time only.
- Don't comment when the child sprays water—just pattern his hands to turn the taps off and remind/help him to wipe hands. Water can be mopped up later.
- Send the child out of the bathroom immediately he has washed and dried his hands.
- Distract the child away from the bathroom by offering him alternative activities.
- Provide opportunities for closely supervised water play outside to show the child how to play appropriately.
- Enlist the aid of bathroom monitors from among the more confident, bossy children.

See also "Non-functional Play".

PART D:
Other Problem Behaviours

Some children behave in quite different and somewhat strange ways that do not obviously follow the behaviour patterns described in Part A. These unusual behaviours may not respond initially to the usual/discussed management techniques.

A child may sit for hours rocking back and forth, she may flick her fingers in front of her face, she may look sideways at patterns on the floor or she may monotonously spin the wheels of a bike or toy car. Another child may continuously pull at her hair, bite her hand, bang her head against the wall or floor or repeatedly hit herself. Still another child may appear overly afraid: sometimes of several things or maybe just one or two. This fear is usually excessive and interferes with her willingness to participate in the world around her.

All of these behaviours—including the repetitive, seemingly purposeless ones, the self-injurious ones as well as the fearful ones—can be classified as severe problem behaviours. All of these behaviours, in the extreme, directly interfere with the child's ability to learn and process information, they prevent the child from using skills learned previously and they constantly disrupt the family.

Parents will often accept these behaviours because past attempts to change them have been largely unsuccessful and distressing for both the child and her parents. Unlike the more usual patterns of problem behaviour, it is often difficult to understand what motivates the child to repeat these extreme behaviours. The situation that immediately precedes the occurrence of the problem behaviours often appears to give little clue as to why the behaviour occurs, and the consequences may not appear to offer any obvious rewards or satisfaction.

These behaviours may not offer a clear and immediate message of communicative intent, but with further study and analysis of the problem behaviour in the contexts where they most commonly occur, it may become possible to offer hypotheses as to why they are occurring.

Current behaviour therapy deals extensively with the treatment of problem behaviour at home and in educational settings such as

preschool and school. There is consensus among educational re-
searchers that, although the elimination of problem behaviour is an
important first step in any remediation program, the focus needs to
be on the longer-term replacement of these behaviours with more
socially acceptable and functional behaviours.

Donellan et al. (1984) suggest that the long-term successful functioning of disabled people depends on expanding their limited response repertoires rather than merely eliminating the problem
behaviours.

> Interventions designed to teach functionally related behav-
> iours in place of aberrant responses make good educational
> sense in this regard. Further, such an approach explicitly
> acknowledges the functional legitimacy of even aberrant
> behaviour and, in so doing, communicates a respectful atti-
> tude concerning the individual exhibiting the behaviour.
> Finally, pragmatic interventions are likely to involve teach-
> ing alternative behaviours maintained by naturally available
> reinforcers, resulting in good generalisation and maintenance.
> (p. 202)

Chapter 11
Repetitive and Self-stimulating Behaviours

Self-stimulating behaviours do not fit the usual models of challenging behaviours. They are highly repetitive and extremely reinforcing to the child.

A child may sit for hours spinning the wheels of a toy car, rocking back and forth, flapping her arms, jumping up and down or spinning around and around. These repetitive, seemingly meaningless activities are difficult to manage, and serve to keep the child isolated and withdrawn from the world around her. The behaviours will continue for long periods, even if no other people are present, and the child may appear unaware of what is happening around her when she is engaged in self-stimulating behaviours. We may, therefore, assume that the behaviours are reinforcing for their own sake, and do not require any external reinforcement.

It is necessary to look closely and carefully at the pattern of these behaviours to discover what motivates the child to repetitively self-stimulate, when the behaviour most often occurs, why it occurs and what is associated with it. Although these behaviours do not obviously follow the usual pattern, by looking closely at what is occurring just before the problem behaviour (situation) and what happens after the behaviour occurs (result), it may be possible to see that some identifiable conditions are usually present when the behaviour occurs. In order to obtain a clearer picture, it is essential to determine the function behind the behaviour—to ask the question, "Why does the behaviour occur?"

Self-stimulating behaviours may be the result of boredom and lack of external stimulation. By providing children with interesting activities, it may be possible to reduce the rate of the self-stimulating behaviour and develop more appropriate play skills.

For example:

- Billy spends hours at home sitting on the floor or on a chair rocking back and forth, especially when he is left alone in the room or the television is on.
- Billy's preschool teacher says that Billy does not rock back and forth at preschool, even when sitting on the floor during group time.

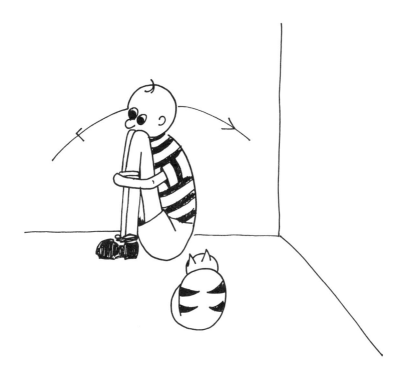

It may be possible to make some general assumptions about Billy's rocking and also to determine what motivates his actions. We know that the behaviour does not occur at preschool when Billy is busily occupied and the setting is very structured. The problem behaviour occurs at home when Billy is not continually stimulated and occupied.

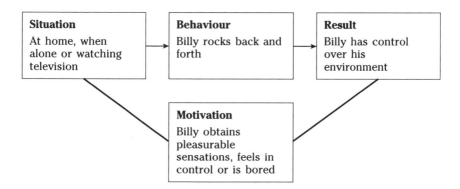

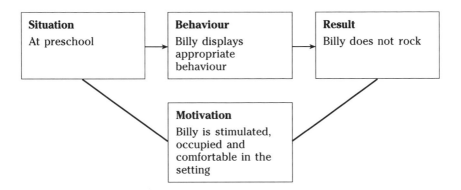

According to Baker et al. (1976), the *situation* may not always be an objective measurable event; sometimes, the child's thoughts and feelings may be seen as causing or at least contributing to the problem behaviour.

Self-stimulating behaviours may occur more often when the child is tired, angry, hungry, excited or bored.

From the example above, we may make the following assumptions about Billy's self-stimulating behaviours.

1   Billy likes to rock when he is left alone and when he watches television.
2   Billy rocks when he is bored.
3   Rocking is a habit that allows Billy to have control over his immediate environment.
4   Billy obtains some pleasurable sensations from rocking.

Often, it is difficult to identify consistent consequences that appear to reinforce the problem behaviour. Once again, however, the consequences that the child derives from problem behaviour may be something internal. Rocking back and forth is self-stimulating: it brings physical sensations that are pleasant.

The feeling of pride and accomplishment, the pleasant physical sensation and also the feeling of control over the environment may all contribute to the reinforcement of the self-stimulating behaviour that keeps the child isolated from the world around her.

A child with limited skills receives few rewards from her environment, and her attempts to participate in activities often lead to failure. By engaging in self-stimulating behaviours, a child is able to block out and ignore the demands of the world around her: she becomes locked in a world of her own. By learning to control the world around her, even if only for short periods of time, she finds a way to deal with the world in general.

Thus, the rewards for self-stimulating behaviour may include both the pleasant physical sensation itself and the predictability and sense of mastery. Because the rewards of these are self-motivating and come from within the child, they cannot readily be changed.

As the child learns to substitute more socially acceptable activities, such as playing appropriately with toys, interacting with other children, singing songs and watching television, her self-stimulating behaviours will generally decrease. This is because such activities are usually incompatible with self-stimulation and, once mastered, can bring greater rewards than the physical sensations of self-stimulation.

Intervention Strategies

Among the approaches used in reducing self-stimulation are:

- Interrupting the behaviour and redirecting the child to a positive alternative. For example, sitting with the child who is rocking and reading a book together.
- Encouraging more socially acceptable, alternative forms of stimulation—using a rocking chair or a swing for children who like to rock; using a hammer board with children who like to flap their arms.
- Using the self-stimulating behaviour as a reinforcer to encourage some other behaviours; for example allowing the child to repetitively flap her piece of string for 2 minutes only after she has completed a certain activity.
- Restructuring the behaviour to a particular setting or a particular time; for example, encouraging the child to throw the ball only outside and only during group games.

Self-stimulation should never be rewarded by attention of any kind. It is always wiser to give lots of attention only when the child is not engaging in self-stimulating behaviour.

The situation in which self-stimulating behaviours occur and the consequences that the child derives from the behaviour may not always be measurable—the child's thoughts and feelings may be involved in the motivation for the behaviour. The best approach for modifying self-stimulating behaviours is to encourage alternative behaviours.

Chapter 12
Self-injurious Behaviours

Self-injurious behaviours, including head-banging, hand-biting, eye-gouging and hair-pulling, are harmful to the child. It is impossible to ignore these behaviours, and a consistent management program is essential in reducing the incidence of them.

Self-injurious behaviours, by definition, inflict physical damage to the child, and cause great stress to family members. They are dramatic, unpleasant to watch, socially unacceptable and, most importantly, they hurt—both the child who may end up with permanent damage and the parents who have to cope under most stressful circumstances.

Self-injurious behaviours require consistent behaviour-management programs to be implemented immediately. It is also important to look beyond the behaviour itself to the message being conveyed by the behaviour. What is the child attempting to communicate through the problem behaviour?

These behaviours are difficult to modify because they do not always appear to conform to any pattern of behaviour. Sometimes, it is possible to understand when and why the behaviours occur; at other times, there appears to be no obvious motivation at all.

When a child head-bangs because one of his obsessive rituals is interfered with, when a child bites his hand because he is prevented from tearing the pages of a book or when a child pulls his hair because he is made to take a bath or clean his teeth, the motivation behind the self-injurious behaviours is obvious. In these incidents, the child's message is loud and clear: "I'm frustrated, leave me alone, I don't want to do this." A longer-term approach to systematically modifying these problem behaviours is to teach the child alternative communicative means for obtaining what he wants, as well as ways of seeking assistance and communicating his feelings.

At other times, there are no clear reasons for the behaviours, and it is difficult to understand how to deal with them. Typically, they attract quick and varied attention. These behaviours also provide the child with some physical sensation that may act as a motivation for the behaviours to continue. Such behaviours also get desired results, because they are difficult to ignore and the child feels in control of the situation.

For example, Billy bangs his head against the wall or on the floor. There does not appear to be any obvious pattern to the behaviour—it happens in different situations, there are no obvious consequences and the child's motivations are unknown. This behaviour appears to be very harmful to Billy and cannot be ignored.

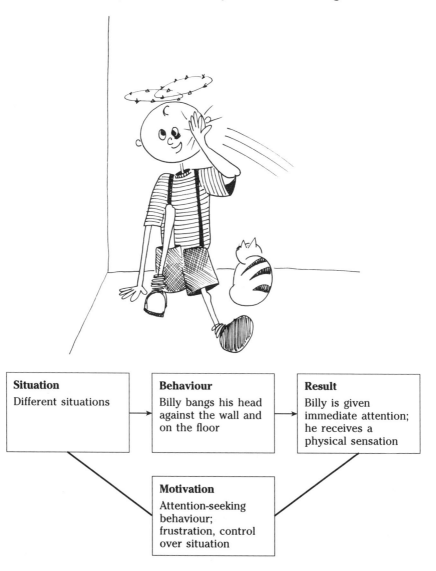

Situation	Behaviour	Result
Different situations	Billy bangs his head against the wall and on the floor	Billy is given immediate attention; he receives a physical sensation

Motivation
Attention-seeking behaviour; frustration, control over situation

This self-injurious behaviour is best managed from a preventative viewpoint. It is not possible to physically stop Billy from banging his head, but it may be possible to recognise the warning signs and distract him from the situation. Most children become more self-injurious when frustrated, angry or anxious. It may be possible to look at when the behaviour mostly occurs and rearrange the situation, so that the child's anxiety and frustration is decreased, or he is encouraged to express his feelings in a more socially acceptable way.

The reactions that a child receives from those around him during self-injurious behaviours is also important. Reactions of anger, fear, surprise or distress may be reinforcing these behaviours. Young children are often unable to differentiate between positive and negative attention, and they respond to all forms of attention.

It is impossible to ignore self-injurious behaviours, but a child should be given minimal attention while engaged in any form of problem behaviour. At the same time, plenty of positive attention should be given to the child for appropriate behaviour. As with other problem behaviours, the child should be taught alternative communicative means for obtaining what he wants and needs, as well as ways of obtaining help and assistance when necessary.

The positive reinforcement used to reward appropriate behaviour will depend upon the child and the situation, but may include non-tangible rewards such as hugs, kisses and verbal praise or, if necessary, more tangible rewards. While attention is kept to a minimum during self-injurious behaviour, the child should be given a firm and concise verbal message—for example, "No head-banging".

To modify Billy's behaviour in the example above, the attention given to Billy when he was head-banging was minimised: this ensured that the behaviour was not reinforced. Billy was praised and given attention when he engaged in alternative, functional activities in order to encourage more appropriate behaviour.

A functional analysis of the problem behaviour led to the formulation of a number of hypotheses to explain possible reasons for the head-banging. These included anxiety, frustration, a lack of appropriate communication skills, hypersensitivity to certain environmental stimuli or some form of chronic pain.

In order to rule out physical factors, a full medical assessment was carried out and a hearing assessment was also completed.

Billy's self-injurious behaviours seemed to be related to the degree of sensory input in his environment. However, it was also noted that the behaviour also increased whenever Billy was frustrated at not being able to adequately communicate his wants and needs.

Direct intervention was provided to teach Billy the skills to communicate in alternative ways through pictorial representations and signing. This enabled Billy to indicate his wants and needs, but also to signal whenever his anxiety or frustration levels increased because of something in his environment. Changes could then be made to the situation or Billy could be redirected to an alternative activity.

Billy was also taught an alternative response of placing his hands over his ears and saying, "Too loud" when the noise levels in his environment became overwhelming. Billy could then be removed from the situation or changes made to accommodate Billy's hypersensitivities. Billy was encouraged to listen to music to keep him calm, and over time, his tolerance of sensory stimulation improved and he developed strategies to help him cope in different situations.

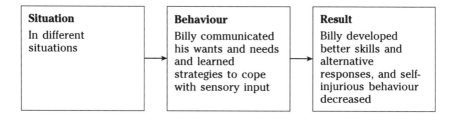

Situation	Behaviour	Result
In different situations	Billy communicated his wants and needs and learned strategies to cope with sensory input	Billy developed better skills and alternative responses, and self-injurious behaviour decreased

All possible rewards should be withheld from the child while he is engaging in any form of self-injurious behaviour. This ensures that there are no pleasant consequences to reinforce the behaviour. Strategies should also be implemented to teach the child more positive ways to deal with his environment. These strategies may include teaching alternative ways of communicating, teaching alternative functional responses in different situations and also modifying the child's environment in order to systematically improve aspects of his lifestyle.

Chapter 13
Fears and Phobias

Some children are overly afraid. They may be afraid of many things or just one or two, including lifts, loud noises, ceiling fans, shopping centres, hairdressers, dogs or even certain toys. The fear is usually excessive: it prevents the child from participating in many normal functions, it is extremely distressing to both the child and other family members and it is also difficult to change or modify.

A child's fears may be mild and short-lived enough so that they do not interfere seriously with social growth. Normally, with a young child, we tend to dismiss these minor fears as unimportant, to find some simple alternative explanation for the behaviour or to reassure the child that there is nothing to be afraid of. This may provide a solution to some minor fears, but does not allow the child to deal with the situation independently, to come to terms with the fear and does not solve the problem of major fears and phobias.

When the child's activity is unnecessarily restricted by fear, however, intervention of some sort is called for. Extreme, irrational fear that is out of proportion to the reality of a situation and leads to automatic avoidance of the feared situation is often called a phobia.

A phobia is a persistent fear of some object or situation that presents no actual danger to the person, or in which the danger is magnified out of all proportion to its actual seriousness.

Fears are learned and maintained in a different way from other problem behaviours, and consequently must be managed in a different way. It is important to note whether a child's anxiety is actually due to the fear of a certain object or situation, or is motivated by something else such as attention or avoidance. When a child is genuinely afraid, she responds to that situation emotionally and has no control over her behaviour.

For example, Mary refuses to use a public toilet when out in the community, because she does not like the automatic hand-dryers.

There are a few different possible explanations:

1   Mary does not know how to use the hand-dryer (and dislikes the hot air blowing on her face and hands). She does not like the noise it makes when activated.

2   Mary enjoys the response she receives when she makes a fuss— she is given lots of attention and is often bribed with offers of favourite foods or activities.

3   Mary is genuinely afraid of the automatic hand-dryer.

We therefore need to answer the following questions before deciding on a program to alter the problem behaviours:

1   Does the child possess the skills to complete the activity successfully?

2   Does the child receive pleasant rewards for behaving inappropriately?

3   Is the child genuinely afraid with no control over her behaviour?

Careful observation of the situation before and the consequences after the occurrence of the fearful behaviour will help to determine whether it is a genuine fear or some other factor that is involved. With a young child, there may be physical signs to show whether the child is actually afraid. She may cry, cling to a familiar adult and become quite agitated.

Sometimes there may be an obvious reason behind a child's fear or phobia—she may have previously been bitten by a dog, frightened by a balloon popping or had the hot air from the hand-dryer blow right in her face. However, often there does not appear to be any obvious history behind the child's fear or phobia. Unlike the usual childhood fears of the dark, strangers or large animals, autistic phobias tend to be of a more bizarre nature. A certain plant, a piece of pipe, a certain room in the house or area of the garden or even a particular member of the family may suddenly and inexplicably become a source of terror or anxiety. Such fears are impossible to cope with as they restrict the movements of the family, not only in the community but also in the home.

> Fears and phobias may be classified as problem behaviours, but they do not usually respond to normal behaviour-management techniques. Regardless of how fears and phobias are acquired, the approaches most commonly used to successfully reduce excessive fears are modelling and systematic desensitisation.

Simply, the aim of any systematic desensitisation program is to decrease the fearful behaviour. At the same time, the aim is to teach the child skills for participating in those situations that previously frightened her. The term "systematic desensitisation" has been applied to a specific approach developed by Wolpe (1961, 1963, 1969). On the assumption that most neurotic patterns are, fundamentally, conditioned anxiety responses, Wolpe designed a method to train a person to remain calm and relaxed in situations that formerly produced anxiety. The central feature of systematic desensitisation procedures involves the child's gradual and repeated approach to the feared object or situation, while ensuring that the child remains calm, and at the same time, engages in an activity that is incompatible with or inhibits anxiety.

For example, a child who is afraid of the hairdresser may be given a packet of lollies to hold and eat while she sits in the hairdressing salon. The gradual approach to the feared object, repeated exposure to it and maintenance of a calm state during exposure to it tends to weaken the conditioned or learned bond between the object and the fear response it elicits.

Wolpe's approach is quite simple and straightforward to implement.

1 *Training in relaxation.* The first step is to encourage the child to relax and to stay calm. This may involve having parents engaged in consciously relaxing the child during periods of anxiety by:
   - modelling;
   - talking slowly and quietly to the child;
   - gently rubbing or stroking the child;
   - sitting quietly with the child and reading a story, watching television together or listening to music.

2 *Arranging the fear into a series of small steps.* It is important to determine what is the least frightening situation for the child and also the most frightening related situation. The situations in between are then filled in from the least to the most fearful, varying the important dimensions and incorporating new aspects as we go. This hierarchy is ranked in descending order according to the amount of fear or anxiety the situations provoke. To begin helping the child overcome her fear or phobia, it is necessary to repeatedly expose her to the *least* fearful situation on the hierarchy. As the child becomes more comfortable in this situation, and exhibits no fear, she is moved on to the next step. We must practise each step until the child displays no fear in that situation.

The important rule to remember is to proceed gradually, not moving to a new step until the child is comfortable with the one before.

The principles behind the systematic desensitisation technique in the treatment of fears and phobias are:

- *Choosing a goal*—what exactly are we aiming to accomplish with the technique?
- *Breaking down the fearful situation into small steps*—from the *least* fearful to the *most* fearful.
- *Proceeding gradually*—not moving to a new step until the child is comfortable with the one before.
- *Rewarding appropriate behaviour*—thus encouraging alternative, more adaptive behaviours to replace the fearful ones.

As well as considering the principles listed above, it is also important to consider:

- *Setting the stage*—it is important to arrange the situation to be minimally distracting and easy to manage. Keep any directions simple.
- *Modelling*—each feared step is more easily mastered if the child sees someone else master that step first.

The procedure for decreasing fearful or phobic behaviour may be summarised as follows:

- Make sure that the behaviour is in fact a fear, and not an attempt to avoid an unwanted situation.
- List the related situations in which the child is afraid, ranging from the least frightening to the most frightening.
- Begin with the least frightening item. Set the stage for success and model what the child should do.
- Ensure that the child is not frightened or anxious in the situation by choosing a time when the child is relaxed and calm, and by providing something for the child to do that is incompatible with the fearful response.
- Remain with the same situation until the child has mastered and shows no fear at all, then move on to the next situation.
- Continue gradually in this way until the child can master all the situations on the hierarchy.

If a child is displaying some minor fears, the suggestions above may be modified slightly to help deal with those fears:

- Modelling—show the child that there is nothing to fear by having someone else do the activity first. Reward the other person for coping with the situation, and then introduce it to the anxious child by making it a turn-taking game.
- Prepare the child in advance by giving her information or demonstrating exactly what is involved.
- Incorporate something pleasant so that the child has something incompatible with the feared situation. This may involve providing a favourite snack, listening to or singing a favourite song or playing a favourite game.
- Ensure that you have complete control of the situation so that everything is prepared and nothing can happen unexpectedly to frighten the child.

- Reassure the child by remaining physically close by, or even making physical contact if appropriate—for example, holding hands.

An example of a program that uses desensitisation and a gradual increase in tolerance to unfamiliar situations is outlined below for the child who is afraid of having her hair cut.

Haircutting

Some children exhibit unnatural fears about having their hair cut. Although this may be classed as a problem behaviour, it requires different management strategies to overcome the child's fear and to prevent the behaviour from recurring. The most common approaches to successfully reduce any excessive fears include modelling and systematic desensitisation. The aim is to decrease the incidence of fearful behaviour, and at the same time, to teach the child skills to be able to comfortably participate in those situations that previously frightened her.

If the child is afraid of having her hair cut, the aim is to gradually show her that the procedure is not threatening, not harmful and, most important, does not hurt. By familiarising the child with the steps involved in the procedure, we can eliminate the child's fear of the unknown and unfamiliar, and show her how to accept the situation and actually participate in it, if not with enjoyment, at least without fear.

Intervention Strategies

- The fearful behaviour is broken down into smaller, less frightening steps.
- A small reward (for example, chocolate) may be given to the child as she achieves each step, building on what was achieved on previous visits.
- Try to follow the same routine each visit and be patient—it may take some time before the child reaches the final steps.
- Prepare the hairdresser before visiting and try to see the same person each time.
- Choose a hairdresser who will be cooperative and positive about the program and who cuts hair quickly.
- Give the hairdresser a bag of sweets to use as rewards, and reward the child immediately after achieving each step.
- The child is exposed to the least fearful step until she feels comfortable and does not display any fear.
- The child is then moved on to the next step.
- Each step is practised until the child shows no fear in the situation.
- An important part of any fear-reducing program is to list steps in any situation in which fear is present from the least to the most frightening, and then to employ a management procedure that is non-threatening to the child. This occurs over a period of time with the child gradually being introduced to each new step as she becomes comfortable with the previous one. A haircutting program may take several months to implement successfully.

Procedure

1   Walk past the hairdresser's; wave to the hairdresser and then buy a reward.
2   Walk into the hairdressing salon.
3   Stay in the salon while enquiries are made; talk to the hairdresser.
4   Walk around the salon.
5   Wait in lounge area.
6   Tolerate being addressed by the hairdresser.
7   Stand up and walk to the appropriate chair.
8   Sit down on the chair.
9   Allow the cloak to be put on.
10 Play with brush, comb, water spray, etc.
11 Allow hair to be combed.
12 Allow water to be sprayed on hair.
13 Allow the hairdresser to approach with scissors.
14 Allow the hairdresser to snip hair at back of head.
15 Allow the hairdresser to cut hair at side of head.
16 Allow the hairdresser to cut hair at front of head.
17 Allow hair to be brushed off.
18 Allow the cloak to be removed.
19 Step down from the chair.
20 Leave hairdresser's—say goodbye or wave to the hairdresser.

During this program, the child should be encouraged to play at home with comb, brush, water spray, toy scissors—use a doll to practise on.

The aim of any systematic desensitisation program is to encourage alternative, socially acceptable behaviours to replace fearful ones. The program should be implemented gradually, and parents and carers must realise that the program will take time, patience and overwhelming optimism if it is to be completely successful.

Rewards

Some form of tangible rewards may be encouraged and actually built into the program from the start. Allowing the child to hold her packet of lollies or her chocolate frog during the program may help to take her mind off the feared situation and also introduce some positive aspect to a situation that is initially quite unfamiliar and threatening to the child. Rewards are individual and may only be classed as reinforcers if they successfully lead to changes in the target behaviour. Some children may not respond to tangible rewards such as lollies and may prefer some other reward system.

Before beginning any management procedure involving the use of rewards, it is essential to determine exactly what rewards are motivating for the child, so that she will be willing to do whatever is requested of her in order to achieve the reward.

Chapter 14

Rituals and Obsessions

Some children may spend many hours of the day involved in repetitive, stereotyped, apparently compulsive activities of some kind or another. The reduction of these problem behaviours is essential because they interfere with the child's ability to learn other skills. They are also extremely disruptive to families.

Although these ritualistic and obsessional behaviours are difficult to eliminate entirely, they may be successfully modified so as to cause less disruption to the child's own life and that of his family. It is important, therefore, to discover an effective method of reducing such behaviours, both for the child's overall growth and development and also for family harmony.

An *obsession* may be defined as repetitive, persistent, preoccupying thoughts about something or someone.

A *ritual* may be defined as the repetitive, stereotyped acts that are an invariable prelude, accompaniment or coda to a specific event.

A *compulsion* may be defined as the repetitive, stereotyped acts that the individual feels he must complete.

Different methods have been tried in the past to reduce these problem behaviours. Many involved aversive techniques that reduced the stereotyped behaviours for a short while, but did not lead to longer-term improvements in the child's behaviour. Punishment should never be used to reduce ritualistic or obsessive behaviours, as the longer-term effectiveness of all forms of punishment are limited. The aim is to teach the child more effective ways of behaving, playing and communicating.

Howlin and Rutter (1987) state that one of the primary aims in any treatment program to reduce obsessive and ritualistic behaviours should be to increase the child's ability to communicate and play appropriately. The desire and the time to engage in problem behaviours will gradually decrease as the child behaves appropriately. As the child's communication and play skills improve, the compulsive need to engage in obsessive and ritualistic behaviours gradually reduces.

For example, if a child is able to learn to communicate better, in a functional way, his obsessive, repetitive questioning behaviours should decrease. This obsessive questioning is usually a sign of insecurity in the child. If a child is taught to play appropriately with toys, his stereotyped, manipulative use of objects, such as lining up toys, spinning wheels and sorting objects according to colour, shape or size, should decrease.

However, although teaching alternative, appropriate means of communicating and playing with objects may produce considerable improvement in behaviour, more direct techniques may also be required to significantly reduce ritualistic and obsessive behaviours.

Obsessions and rituals can become very intrusive in a child's everyday life, they are very time-consuming, they interfere with the child's ability to learn and process information from the world around him and they can place some heavy burdens on the child and other family members. It is possible to deal successfully with these problem behaviours, but it is extremely hard work and can be quite distressing for all concerned. It requires careful consideration and lots of thought before embarking on any major procedure to reduce obsessive and ritualistic behaviours.

Some obsessive behaviours begin in the young child as fairly mild problems that escalate over time as no attempts are made to stop them. As the child gets older, these rigid behaviours become stronger and increase to include new situations and objects. They also become more noticeable, embarrassing and disruptive.

> If the ritualistic behaviours have gradually increased in intensity over time, the most effective method of dealing with these behaviours involves a *progressively graded introduction to change*. In some cases, this involves restricting the child's opportunities to indulge in these behaviours; in other cases, it involves systematic modification of the behaviours themselves.

Many children spend most of their time in repetitive, stereotyped, apparently compulsive activities of one kind or another. These may include the endless lining up of objects, repetitive opening and closing of doors, obsessively touching certain objects or performing certain rituals in all self-help tasks. The aim of a management procedure is to reduce their severity or their frequency.

For example, Billy would spend hours repetitively opening and closing cupboard doors. If his parents put locks on the cupboard doors, Billy would move on to the oven door, microwave, fridge and dishwasher doors. Attempts by his parents to interfere with this obsession, to lock the doors or stop Billy from touching them would result in extreme distress.

Initially, it is necessary to restrict the child's opportunities to indulge in the behaviour. Billy was allowed to open and close the doors in all rooms except the bathroom. Billy loved to take a bath and was only allowed to have a bath if he did not open and close the bathroom cupboard doors. This procedure was gradually extended to include the loungeroom (no television if he opened and closed cupboard doors), parents' bedroom (he was not allowed in bed for a cuddle), and eventually, in the kitchen (no snacks if he opened and closed the kitchen doors). Billy was allowed to open and close the cupboard doors in his bedroom, but this gradually decreased as he did not particularly like to spend all his time alone in his bedroom.

It is not really possible to eliminate all ritualistic, obsessive behaviours entirely. The aim is to reduce these problem behaviours to a manageable level so that they do not interfere with the rest of the family or with the child's enjoyment in more normal, appropriate activities.

For example, Mary would spend all her time lining up marbles. She became very distressed if she was prevented from doing this, or if her lines were interfered with or the marbles would not remain still.

Progressively graded introduction to change was used in this case to gradually decrease the number of marbles that Mary lined up. Her parents insisted that the number of marbles in the line at any one time was gradually lowered. Instead of spending her time lining up 100 marbles or more, the maximum allowed was reduced to 75 marbles. This was further reduced to 50, then to 30, to 20 and eventually to five. Although this resulted in little lines of five marbles dotted around the house, it greatly reduced the distress when the lines were broken, and eventually her obsession with the marbles faded.

Resistance to change in the environment may also be dealt with using graded-change techniques. Many children are extremely distressed by minor changes in their environment, such as a sofa being moved, a door being left open or the removal of a picture. In such cases of resistance to change, barely perceptible alterations in the positioning of objects is generally the first step in modifying the behaviour. Once the child is able to tolerate these minor changes, more and more changes are gradually introduced, and the child is encouraged to tolerate them. Whenever possible, the changes should be predictable for the child. Sometimes, it may be possible to explain to a child about possible changes in advance. If alterations are predicted in such a way, the child is generally able to tolerate subsequent changes more readily.

Sleeping problems have also been dealt with effectively by the use of graded-change techniques. For example, Billy insisted that his mother remain in the room with him at night. Whenever she attempted to leave the room, Billy screamed loudly enough to wake the neighbours. The only way that his mother could get any sleep was to sleep in the bed with Billy.

The graded-change technique involved the mother systematically removing herself from the child's bedroom. Initially, Billy's mother slept on a mattress in Billy's bedroom. This was placed immediately next to Billy's bed so that his mother was within easy reach of Billy if he woke during the night. Gradually, the mattress was moved away from Billy's bed. His mother could speak to and touch him if he woke, but could no longer cuddle him. Gradually, the mattress was moved closer to the door. If he woke, she could comfort him verbally, but could no longer touch him. These changes were accepted by Billy, and after 2 months, his mother's mattress was placed in the hallway between his bedroom and hers. After 3 months, Billy's mother had returned to her own bed, and if Billy woke during the night, he was easily pacified by his mother calling to him and encouraging him to go back to sleep.

Although ritualistic and obsessional behaviours are difficult to eliminate entirely, they can be modified to cause less distress and disruption to family life. It is important to ensure that these problem behaviours never entirely take over other aspects of the child's functioning. The longer an obsessional behaviour has persisted, the longer it will take to successfully modify it. It is important, therefore, for parents to be aware of potential obsessional activities that may replace an original obsession, and to restrict these immediately.

Conclusion

This book was written to assist parents and other carers to minimise and prevent problem behaviours of children with disabilities, both at home and in the community. Behaviour management involves analysing the problem behaviours and adjusting the child's environment to reduce the frequency and the severity of the behaviours. This book also provides information about management and teaching programs to develop alternative, functional behaviours so that the young child with a disability can live in the community and have control over her own life.

In the past, the focus of most behaviour-management programs was on using aversive methods such as punishment, time out and physical restraint to eliminate or suppress problem behaviour. The benefits of these methods were short term and were of questionable morality in terms of current research and theory.

Current programs aim to prevent problem behaviour occurring as much as possible by creating a caring, supportive and secure environment for the child. When problem behaviour persists, the emphasis is upon looking beyond the behaviour itself to the wider context or situation in which the behaviour occurs.

A behaviour-management program involves:

- developing a plan to systematically improve the child's lifestyle. This includes introducing structure and routine into the child's day; ensuring that activities are age-appropriate and interesting; expanding the child's choices; providing opportunities to socialise; and improving the child's control over her own life.

- providing the child with adequate skills in all areas of development, especially in the areas of communication, play and socialisation. The child should be able to communicate either verbally or non-verbally her basic wants, needs and emotions; interact with other children to the degree that she feels comfortable with; play with a wide range of toys and equipment at her current level of functioning; and complete some basic self-help tasks as independently as possible.

- implementing a planned procedure that allows parents and carers to deal with the actual problem behaviour in context as soon as it occurs. This may involve redirecting the child, ignoring the behaviour, removing an object from the child, verbally directing the child to stop the behaviour or physically blocking the behaviour.
- encouraging more appropriate, alternative behaviours that are incompatible with the problem behaviour.

"There is growing awareness among educators that the long-term successful functioning of persons with severe handicaps depends on expanding their limited response repertoires rather than simply eliminating their inappropriate behaviours." (Donellan et al., 1984)

Bibliography

Alberto, P. A. and Troutman, A. C. (1982): *Applied Behaviour Analysis for Teachers*, Ohio, Charles E. Merrill.

Baker, B. L., Brightman, A. J., Heifetz, L. J., Murphy, D. M. (1976): *Behaviour Problems*, Illinois, Research Press.

Coleman, J. C., Butcher, J. N. and Carson, R. C. (1980): *Abnormal Psychology and Modern Life*, 6th edn, Glenview, Illinois, Scott, Foresman & Co.

Donellan, A. M., Miranda, P. L., Mesaros, R. A. and Fassbender, L. L. (1984): "A Strategy for Analysing the Communicative Functions of Aberrant Behaviour", *Journal of the Association for Persons with Severe Handicaps*, vol. 9, no. 3, 201–12.

Evans, I. M. and Meyer, L. J. (1985): *An Educative Approach to Behaviour Problems: A Practical Decision Model for Interventions with Severely Handicapped Learners*, Baltimore, Paul H. Brookes.

Foxx, R. M. (1982a): *Decreasing Behaviour of Severely Retarded and Autistic Persons*, Illinois, Research Press.

—— (1982b): *Increasing Behaviour in Severely Retarded and Autistic Persons*, Illinois, Research Press.

Foxx, R. M. and Azrin, N. H. (1972): "Restitution: A Method of Eliminating Aggressive-disruptive Behaviour of Retarded and Brain-damaged Patients", *Behaviour Research and Therapy*, 10, 15–27.

—— (1973): "The Elimination of Autistic Self-stimulatory Behaviour by Overcorrection", *Journal of Applied Behaviour Analysis*, 6, 1–14.

Howlin, P. and Rutter, M. (1987): *Treatment of Autistic Children*, London, John Wiley & Sons.

MacDonald, L., Uditsky, B., McDonald, S. and Swan, Rose (1992): "A Training Program for Parents of Developmentally-Delayed Children with Behaviour Problems", *Journal of Practical Approaches to Developmental Handicap*, Alberta, Alberta Social Services and Community Health.

Meyer, L. J. and Evans, I. M. (1989): *Nonaversive Intervention for Behaviour Problems: A Manual for Home and Community*, Baltimore, Paul H. Brookes.

Rauch, A. (ed.) (1993): *Behaviour Management: An Approach for the 90s*, Newcastle, ASSID Publications, University of Newcastle.

Rutter, M. and Schopler, E. (1987): "Autism and Pervasive Developmental Disorders: Concepts and Diagnostic Issues", in Rutter, M., Tuma, A. and Lann, I. (eds) *Assessment and Classification in Child and Adolescent Psychiatry*, New York, Guilford Press.

Stancliffe, R. (1989): *Prevention and Management of Challenging Behaviour*, Sydney, Autistic Association of NSW.

Sulzer-Azaroff, B. and Mayer, G. R. (1977): *Applying Behaviour Analysis Procedures with Children and Youth*, New York, Holt, Rinehard and Winston.

Wolpe, J. (1958): *Psychotherapy by Reciprocal Inhibition*, Stanford, Stanford University Press.

—— (1961): "The Systematic Desensitisation Treatment of Neuroses", *Journal of Nervous Mental Diseases* 132, 189–203.

—— (1969): *The Practice of Behaviour Therapy*, New York, Pergamon.

—— (1963): "Qualitative Relationships in the Systematic Desensitisation of Phobias", *American Journal of Psychiatry*, 119, 1062.

Glossary

A

Absconding: persistent attempts to escape from a particular situation or place.

Abstract thinking: the ability to think about concepts that are not concrete, and so cannot be seen or heard.

Abnormal: maladaptive behaviour detrimental to the individual and/or the group.

Acquisition: to obtain a new or additional characteristic, trait or ability.

Adaptability: flexibility in meeting changed circumstances or demands.

Adaptation to environment: accepting change in, and intrusion from, the surrounding world, and changing one's own behaviour or opinions to follow.

Adolescence: the period between the onset of puberty and the cessation of physical growth.

Advocate: a person who acts on behalf of another.

Affective disorders: disorders of feeling or mood—an emotional disorder that colours one's outlook on life, usually characterised by either elation or depression.

Aggression: attacking others physically or verbally; hostile, injurious or destructive behaviour or outlook.

Alternative Communication System: a method of communication as a substitute for verbal language, it may include signing, gestures, pointing to photos, line drawings or written words. (*See* Augmentative communication system)

Anecdotal recording: a factual account of a child's behaviour.

Antecedent: a situation or incident happening before the occurrence of a challenging behaviour, which may be partially the cause of the behaviour.

Anxiety: a feeling of uneasiness, apprehension or dread.

Aphasia: acquired language disorder caused by brain damage, resulting in partial or complete impairment of language comprehension, formulation and use for communication. For example:

Auditory aphasia: inability to comprehend spoken words.

Formulation aphasia: inability to formulate sentences correctly. Confusion occurs in relationships and tenses rather than in words themselves.

Apraxic: loss of the ability to voluntarily produce expressive motor movements—a medical term reflecting an abnormality of the central nervous system.

Appropriate: something that is suitable or compatible.

Articulation: the manner in which speech sounds are produced—how elements of words are spoken, to improve or affect the clarity of speech.

Asperger's syndrome: a condition with strong similarities to autism, but where the individual's early linguistic development is not delayed and may even be advanced. Language, however, is still used in a stilted and stereotyped manner. Intellectually, individuals with Asperger's syndrome usually function in the normal range of ability. May be considered at the high end of the autism spectrum.

Assessment: either a test or an observation that determines a child's strengths and weaknesses in a particular area of development.

Association: a strategy for increasing long-term memory—a new event or events to be remembered are deliberately linked to similar and easily recalled categories or events.

Ataxia: lack of coordination of voluntary muscles, symptomatic of one variety of cerebral palsy.

Atypical: different from the norm or average.

Attention deficit disorder (ADD): the essential features of attention deficit disorder are developmentally inappropriate degrees of inattention, impulsiveness and hyperactivity. People with the disorder generally display some disturbances in each of these areas, but to varying degrees. However, it is not necessary to display all of the above behaviours for diagnosis.

Auditory: perceived through hearing.

Augmentative communication system: a method of communication used to supplement verbal communication or to assist people to understand and use verbal communication systems more easily. (*See* Alternative communication system)

Autism: a rare developmental disability characterised by severe problems in communication and behaviour, and an inability to relate to people in a normal manner. It is evident before 30 months of age. Diagnosis requires skilled medical and psychological evaluation. With skilled intervention and support, people with autism can develop their abilities and participate in community life.

Autistic savant: an exceedingly rare condition in which persons with serious mental handicaps have spectacular areas of brilliance that stand in stark, markedly incongruous contrast to the handicap.

Aversive: uncomfortable; something that will act as a disincentive when paired with an inappropriate behaviour; rewards for appropriate behaviours should also be given consecutively.

Aversive stimulus: a negative stimulus that has the effect of decreasing the strength of a behaviour when it is presented as a consequence of that behaviour; a stimulus that the person will actively work to avoid; an unpleasant object or event.

Avoidance behaviour: staying away from or doing something to avoid being punished.

B

Backward chaining: rewarding small parts of the whole behaviour or skill, in the order in which the behaviour or skill is performed, beginning with the final step in the behaviour or skill. As each successive step is mastered and performed along with the previous step, reinforcement is shifted to the next step in the chain.

Baseline: an observation of a behaviour before intervention is undertaken.

Behavioural assessment: a technique to determine the functional relationships between an individual's behaviour and environmental stimuli.

Behaviour management: adapting a person's challenging behaviours, and improving or training acceptable behaviours and skills in the context of the whole person and the situation in which the person is functioning.

Behaviour modification: systematic, consistent efforts to change an individual's behaviour. Carefully planned consequences for specific behaviours are designed to help a learner develop new and more appropriate responses to situations and experiences.

Behavioural contract: a contract, often between family members, stipulating privileges and responsibilities. Used with more able persons.

Behavioural intervention: the control or change of challenging behaviours.

Behaviour therapy: a scientifically based approach to modifying and shaping behaviour by identifying and manipulating the triggers and reinforcements of specific behaviours.

Behavioural objective: identifies exactly what the teacher will do, provide or restrict; describes the learner's observable behaviour and defines how well the learner must perform.

C

Case study: assessment information on a specific individual.

CAT scans: stands for computed axial tomography. This is an advanced form of X-ray that is especially useful in obtaining pictures of the brain.

Central nervous system (CNS): the brain and spinal cord.

Centre-based education: a program that focuses on exposing children to an educationally stimulating environment outside the home in attempts to facilitate the development of intellectual competence.

Cerebral palsy: a disorder that is the result of damage to or maldevelopment of the brain.

Childhood schizophrenia: severe disorder of childhood, distinguishable from autism. Characterised by bizarre behaviour patterns, distortions of thinking and abnormal perceptions.

Chaining: a procedure to teach complex behaviours by linking together a series of responses already in the child's repertoire. Rewarding small parts of the whole behaviour or skill in the order in which the behaviour or skill is performed.

Challenging behaviour: any behaviour outside the range of socially acceptable and non-descriptive behaviour; any behaviour that requires intervention to change or modify it.

Classical autism (Kanner-syndrome): the original definition of autism: "inability to develop relationships with people, delay in speech acquisition, non-communicative use of speech after it develops, delayed echolalia, pronominal reversal, repetitive and stereotyped play activities, an obsessive insistence on the maintenance of sameness, lack of imagination, good role memory and a normal physical appearance" (Rutter and Schopler, 1987).

Chromosomes: thread-like bodies in the nucleus of the cell. Structural arrangements of genes. Most human body cells contain 23 pairs of chromosomes. Genes are responsible for many physical and mental characteristics.

Chronological age (CA): a child's actual age in years and months.

Classification: sorting, matching or otherwise grouping things by their distinguishing characteristics.

Cognition: mental processes, including perception, memory and reasoning by which one acquires knowledge, solves problems and makes plans.

Communication: the encoding of a message to stimulate meaning in the mind of another, and the accurate decoding of the intended meaning of others; entails an exchange of ideas and intentions.

Communication skills: the ability to express oneself to others, and understand the messages others are trying to convey.

Community access: having the individual actively participate in normal, outside activities that are part of everyday life.

Comprehension: understanding what a word or series of words means; the association of sound sequences with appropriate concepts.

Compliance: yielding; making one's desires conform to the wishes of others but without changing one's private attitudes.

Compic: a universal series of representational line drawings that may be used as a form of communication.

Conductive hearing loss: impairment in the mechanical transmission of sound waves through the outer and middle ear.

Concrete thinking: ability to deal effectively with practical or concrete situations and relationships; no understanding or production of abstract thought.

Confidentiality: privacy: records and other information about children should not be shown to anyone other than those who have been approved to have the information. Parental consent in writing must be obtained before information can be released to other individuals or facilities. There is a commitment on the part of a professional person to keep confidential information he or she obtains from a client.

Congenital: existing at birth or before birth, but not necessarily hereditary.

Consequences: circumstances that occur following a behaviour, intended to affect the incidence of the behaviour.

Consistency: giving the same message to the person in different situations and with different people involved.

Contingency: relationship, usually causal, between two events in which one is usually followed by the other.

Contingent reinforcement: reinforcement that depends on a specific response.

Continuous reinforcement: reward or reinforcement given regularly after each correct response.

Coping strategies: useful techniques that will be effective in assisting a person to cope in a particular situation.

Counsellor: a person with skills to assist families deal with social and welfare issues.

Criterion-referenced tests: tests or observations that compare a child's performance on a particular task to a standard established for that specific task. Such tests identify what the child can and cannot do.

Cues: indications to remind people to do something, or of having to do it in a certain way; can be verbal, gestural, physical or expressed by the facial expression or body language.

Curriculum: all the specific features of a master teaching plan that have been chosen by a particular teacher for his or her classroom. Curriculum may vary widely from school to school, but each curriculum reflects the skills, tasks and behaviours that a teaching program has decided are important for children to acquire.

"Cut-off" behaviour: attempts to reduce intrusion or input from the environment by employing certain behaviour—for example, self-stimulating behaviour, withdrawal, ritualistic and repetitive behaviours.

Current level of functioning: description of a child's abilities in different key areas at a given time.

D

Daily living skills: skills that enable us to function in situations we meet in everyday life.

Data collection: the gathering of relevant information in order to determine whether a particular program is working or not.

Degree of disability: a measurement of the present impact of a handicap on a person, generally accepted to range from mild through moderate to severe and profound.

Demonstration: modelling a task or activity to indicate to a person how it should be done; the person needs imitation skills to be able to repeat the demonstration.

Descriptive recording: recording briefly in written form what happened before, during and after certain incidents in order to determine some consistent pattern of behaviour.

Desensitisation: a program of support to enable a person to come to accept an object, person or situation previously feared or not tolerated for some reason; the technique involves supporting the person through successive small steps toward exposure to the particular problem.

Developmental delay (disability): a condition that originates in childhood and results in an identifiable delay in mental or physical development compared with established norms. Children are referred to as developmentally delayed rather than "impaired" or "retarded".

Developmental therapy: speech therapy, occupational therapy and physiotherapy all assist development to occur.

Deviant behaviour: behaviour that deviates markedly from the average or norm.

Diagnosis: an effort to find the cause and extent of a specific problem by observation and assessment.

Direct observation: a method of behavioural assessment in which a person's behaviour is observed in a practical situation.

Disabled: reduced functioning as a result of a physical deficit or a significant problem in learning or social adjustment; sometimes used more narrowly to refer to physical deficits or crippling conditions.

Discrete response: a behaviour that has a clearly defined beginning and end. Throwing, biting and hitting are all examples of discrete responses.

Disordered: reduced functioning, particularly in academic achievement (for example, learning disorders), social adjustment (behaviour disorders) or oral language use (for example, speech or language disorders).

Discrimination: ability to interpret and respond differently to two or more similar stimuli.

Distraction: removing a person's attention from an inappropriate behaviour or situation that is making a behaviour worse.

Dominant gene: a gene whose hereditary characteristics prevail in the offspring.

Down syndrome: a form of mental retardation with noticeable physical signs—slanted eyes with entire lid fold, thick tongue, stubby limbs and fingers, sparse, fine, straight hair—induced by a genetic anomaly, usually trisomy in the 21st chromosomes.

DSM-IIIR: the present revision of the *Diagnostic and Statistical Manual of Mental Disorders*, published by the American Psychiatric Association. DSM-III was preceded by DSM-I and DSM-II.

Drug therapy: the use of medication to control behaviour and reduce the symptoms of autism.

Due process: a right of a citizen to protest before any government acts to deprive him or her of the rights to life, liberty or property.

Duration recording: a behavioural-assessment procedure used to measure the length of time a target behaviour occurs; data may be recorded in seconds, minutes or percentages.

Dyslexia: partial inability to read, or to understand what one reads, silently or aloud, usually, but not always, associated with brain impairment.

E

Early intervention: provision of special assistance, treatment and education to infants and preschool children and their families, where children have a developmental delay. Early intervention programs are essential for children with a disability.

Echolalia: the repetition of sounds, words, phrases, sentences and even whole conversations the person has heard before. The person may even use the accent and intonation patterns of the original speech when repeating it. It may not be used in its correct context but is increasingly recognised to have a communicative function. Echolalia can be immediate, delayed (repeated hours, days or even years after initially being heard), or mitigated (altered in a systematic way showing some awareness of linguistic mechanisms).

Egocentric: preoccupation with one's own concerns and relative insensitivity to the concerns of others.

Elective mutism: a disorder characterised by mutism in specific situations (that is, the child speaks only in certain circumstances). Often, there is evidence of extreme shyness and sensitivity.

Empathy: the ability to understand and to some extent share the state of mind of another person.

EEG (electro-encephalogram): a record of the spontaneous electrical activity of the brain, obtained by attaching electrodes to the scalp and greatly amplifying the voltage changes. Commonly referred to as record of "brain waves".

Encephalitis: inflammation of the brain.

Encopresis: a disorder defined by having bowel movements in one's clothing —incontinence of faeces not due to organic defect or illness.

Enuresis: bedwetting; involuntary discharge of urine usually during sleep at night.

Environment: everything the child encounters. The rooms, furniture, toys, the opportunity to experience new and different places and the behaviours of those around the person constitute the environment.

Epilepsy: convulsive disturbance of the electrical activity of the brain causing loss of consciousness, abnormal physical or sensory reactions.

Evaluation: the process of making value judgements based on behavioural information about the effectiveness of a program in meeting the needs of the children enrolled.

Exceptional: deviation from the norm, either by higher than average or lower than average performance or ability.

Expressive language: the method by which information is transmitted to another person—may be verbal, by signs or pictorial, etc.

Extinction: decreasing a behaviour by removing the reward a person is achieving through the behaviour, or through controlling the antecedent to the behaviour.

Eye contact: keeping attention on the situation and the people involved: maintaining interest and attention during a conversation by actually looking directly at the other person involved.

F

Facial expression: indicates the impact of what is being said to a person; we alter what we say according to our observation of facial expression in others; we have to be able to use and interpret facial expression for a successful conversation to continue.

Facilitated communication: Communicating via a keyboard or message board with assistance from another person (facilitator) supporting hand or arm. Controversial—not clearly proven via research to date.

Fading: reducing the number of reminders or prompts given, until the individual can perform a target activity with no cues at all; fading should occur slowly, at a rate suitable for the individual, in order to maintain the target behaviour, but not to allow the individual to become too reliant on the cues.

Family therapy: form of interpersonal therapy focusing on the relationships within the family.

Feedback: information about the effect of internal physiological processes or social consequences from a source that is useful in regulating behaviour.

Fine motor skills: small muscle skills such as grasping, eye–hand co-ordination, writing; activities involving the use of the fingers and hands.

Fragile-X syndrome: an inherited chromosomal abnormality that leads to learning difficulties and mental handicap. So called because the X chromosome is fragile

Fraternal twins: dizygotic twins, fertilised by separate germ cells, thus not having the same genetic inheritance. May be of the same or opposite sex.

Frequency: an array of measurements from lowest to highest, or indicating the number of times a behaviour or event occurs.

Frustration: any state of affairs that prevents a person from obtaining a desired goal; the condition of being thwarted in some purpose.

Functional skills: skills to assist the person to cope independently in everyday situations.

G

Gag reflex: the normal desire to cough or vomit when choking or when a foreign body is swallowed.

Generalisation: the carrying over of a learned skill or behaviour into another situation or set of circumstances.

1 *Stimulus generalisation*: the extension or carry-over of trained behaviours (for example, words, signs, gestures) to new situations (with different persons, in different settings with different stimuli and removed in time from training).

2 *Response generalisation*: the use of newly acquired skills to expand existing repertoires.

Genetics: the branch of biology concerned with the principles of heredity.

Genetic counselling: counselling prospective parents concerning the probability of their having affected offspring as a result of genetic defects; understanding behaviour in terms of its hereditary origins and developmental history.

Global: perceived as a whole without attempt to distinguish separate parts or functions.

Graded change: a systematic, progressively graded introduction to changes in the routine or situation in order to allow the child to cope with change without undue stress and anxiety.

Grammar:

1 a theory or hypothesis about the organisation of language in the mind of speakers of that language—the underlying knowledge that permits understanding and production of language.

2 language usage relative to some standard of linguistic etiquette.

Grand mal epilepsy: a form of epilepsy characterised by loss of consciousness and violent convulsions.

Gross motor skills: activities using large muscles such as running, climbing, throwing and jumping.

Group therapy: therapeutic intervention with two or more individuals at the same time.

Guardian: someone legally appointed to protect another person's property and rights when the person is incapable of managing his or her own affairs.

H

Habituation: the process whereby an individual's response to the same stimulus lessens with repeated presentations.

Handedness: referring to the hand preference of an individual.

Hand–eye coordination: ability of the hand and eye to perform easily together.

Heredity: genetic transmission of characteristics from parents to their children.

Hierarchy of needs: the concept that needs arrange themselves in a hierarchy in terms of importance, or from the most basic biological needs to those psychological needs concerned with self.

High-risk group: group showing great vulnerability to physical or mental disorders.

Holding therapy: a technique of "socialising" the person with autism through planned, extended sessions of physical contact.

Home-based program: a program that works with children and families in the familiar home environment.

Hydrocephalus: a condition produced by an accumulation of cerebrospinal fluid in the cranial cavity of the skull. When this happens early in life, the head enlarges. The condition is associated with mental retardation.

Hyperactivity: a disorder of childhood characterised by overactivity, restlessness and distractability.

Hypoactivity: insufficient motor activity, characterised by lethargy.

Hypothalamus: a key structure at the base of the brain that controls many emotional and motivational processes.

Hypothesis: a testable proposition advanced to explain or predict certain facts.

I

Identification: the process of finding and screening individuals to determine if they might benefit from specialised services.

Idiot savant: a person with mental retardation who can perform unusual mental feats, usually involving music or manipulation of numbers.

Ignoring: withdrawal of attention.

Imitation skills: the ability to watch, register and copy actions, speech etc. used by another person.

Implement: establish or carry out.

Impulsivity: initiation of sudden action without sufficient forethought or prudence to determine the consequences.

Inappropriate behaviour: behaviour that is not acceptable for a particular situation, given a person's age or intellectual ability: behaviour that generally makes the person stand out as being different from others.

Inappropriate fears: fear or anxiety in situations or in the presence of objects or persons that are not normally anxiety-producing to people of the same age and intellectual functioning.

Incidental learning: learning that takes place without the intent to learn or in the absence of formal instructions.

Incompatible response: a response that cannot take place at the same time as another response; for example, sitting and standing are incompatible responses.

Independent variable: a factor whose effects are being examined in an experiment; it is manipulated in some way while the other variables are held constant. Any variable that serves as a basis for making a prediction.

Individualised Educational Program (IEP): an individualised written plan that is developed and maintained for each special-needs child. The IEP must state the child's current level of educational performance, annual goals, short-term instructional objectives, specific services to be provided, dates services are to be provided and criteria for evaluation.

Infantile autism: *see* Autism.

Inhibition: conscious restraint of impulse or desire.

Initiate: action involved in beginning a series of events; acting independently.

Innate: inborn; inherent within an individual.

Inner language: the language in which thinking occurs. The process of internalising and organising experiences that can be expressed by symbols.

Instructional objectives: definitions of specific accomplishments to be achieved.

Integration: the inclusion of a person with a handicap into an environment in which most people do not have the same level of handicap or have no handicap at all; integration should be supported, if necessary, done gradually and should be for the benefit of the person with the handicap.

Intelligence: pertaining to ability to learn, reason and adapt.

Intelligence quotient (IQ): measurement of "intelligence" expressed as a number or position on a scale. Comparable to the term "intellectual level". Measurement is derived from the administration of standardised tests of different aspects of cognition and language.

Interaction: a relationship between systems such that events taking place in one system influence events taking place in the other. A social relationship between people such that individuals mutually influence each other.

Interdisciplinary approach: integration of various scientific disciplines in understanding, assessing, treating and preventing mental disorders.

Intermittent reinforcement: reinforcement given randomly rather than after every response.

Interval recording: a behavioural assessment procedure in which the observation period is divided into equal time intervals; it permits relatively precise measurement of low and medium rates of responding.

Intellectual disability: a limitation or slowness in individuals' general ability to learn that affects how they function within society. The accepted definition refers to significantly below-normal general intellectual functioning existing concurrently with deficits in adaptive behaviour, manifested before 18 years of age.

Itinerant teacher: a teacher who moves about a school district or several schools and schedules children for teaching periods; children leave their regular classrooms to work individually with the teacher.

J

Jargon: an unintelligible form of speech that appears to hold some meaning to the person using it; also a form used by professional groups to describe specialised terminology or concepts.

K

Kanner-type (classical) autism: *see* Classical autism (Kanner-syndrome).

Kinesthetic: sensory impressions that come from the joints, muscles and tendons, and provide information about the positions and movements of parts of the body.

Klinefelter syndrome: a disorder of males in which an extra X chromosome keeps the testicles small at puberty, disrupts hormonal balance and is likely to cause sterility.

L

Labelling: a classification process where individuals are categorised by some group of similar characteristics.

Landau Kleffner syndrome: a disorder of children associated with acquired aphasia and widespread epileptic abnormalities (spikes and spike waves) in the EEG. In the majority of cases, the onset is between the ages of 4 and 7. The typical language deficit is in auditory comprehension. Deafness is often thought to be present. Progressive aphasia follows. Written language is usually less affected.

Language: a system of vocal or graphic symbols providing people with a method of interacting and communicating. Non-verbal language involves signing and using physical symbols to enable individuals to communicate.

Language sample: the recorded transcription of oral communication; often used to assess language competence.

Latency recording: a behavioural-assessment procedure in which the time that elapses between stimulus and response initiation is recorded.

Learning: a fairly permanent change in behaviour that occurs as a result of experience.

Learning disability: a failure to develop a normal capacity to learn, usually of some specific skill. It is definitionally linked to a lack of progress at school.

Learning strategies: activities undertaken by an individual to cope with the requirements of a task or to solve a problem.

Least restrictive environment: an American concept in Public Law 94-142 that requires handicapped children to be educated with non-handicapped peers in regular educational settings to the maximum extent appropriate; the educational setting that is closest to full participation in the regular classroom, but that still meets the exceptional student's special needs.

Level of functioning: the age level at which a child is able to perform cognitive tasks rather than her chronological age.

Linguistic competence: possession of the rules of language; the ability to create and understand an indefinitely large number of expressions.

Linguistics: the study of human communication in its various aspects, including phonology, phonetics, morphology, syntax and semantics.

Literal thinking: accepting things exactly as written or said without allowing for abstract interpretations—for example, in figures of speech.

Locomotor: pertaining to movement from one location to another such as walking, crawling, rolling etc.

Long-term memory: a memory system of long duration, following after short-term memory.

Long-term objective: a programming aim that may take some time to achieve.

Longitudinal study: research study that follows individuals over a long period of time to investigate changes in development.

M

Macrocephaly: an abnormally large head; a condition that causes retardation.

Mainstreaming: a system of integrating disabled students into regular classes, providing for their special needs through individualised instruction, tutoring or spending a portion of their day with a resource or special teacher.

Maintenance: the ability to perform a response over time, even after systematic applied behaviour procedures have been withdrawn.

Makaton vocabulary: a specifically designed vocabulary to provide a controlled method of teaching British sign language to children and adults with intellectual disability. Used in conjunction with Australian signing system.

Maladaptive behaviour: behaviour that is detrimental to the well-being of the individual and/or the group, and shows that the individual is not adapting in an appropriate way to the environment.

Management strategies: ideas and actions that, when put into practice, will allow a child's inappropriate behaviours to be successfully managed.

Masturbation: self-stimulation of genitals for sexual gratification.

Maturation: the process of development and body change resulting from heredity rather than learning.

Mean length of utterance (MLU): a method of quantifying language development; it is most reliable as an index of linguistic competence when children produce sentences with fewer than 4 words. Average length of morphemes in a child's utterance.

Measurement: the assignment of numerals to objects or events according to rules.

Medical model: a view of mental disorders that assumes that they are diseases similar to the traditional physical diseases treated by medical practitioners.

Medication: prescribed chemical intervention for illness or behaviour.

Memory: the ability to store and retrieve or demand previously experienced sensations and perceptions, even when the stimulus that originally evoked them is no longer present. Also referred to as "imagery" and "recall".

Memory span: the number of related or unrelated items that can be recalled immediately after presentation.

Mental age (MA): a scale unit indicating level of intellectual functioning in relation to chronological age.

Mental retardation: a condition of significantly below-average intellectual functioning and of deficits in adaptive behaviour that are first manifested during childhood.

Microcephaly: an abnormally small head and brain area caused by disease, trauma or a pair of defective recessive genes; a condition that brings mental retardation.

Minimal brain dysfunction: a mild or minimal neurological abnormality that causes learning difficulties in the child with near-average intelligence.

Modelling: a form of learning in which the individual learns by watching someone else perform the desired response.

Modification: any change in structure or function due to internal, external or hereditary influences.

Monozygotic twins: twins who develop from a single egg, hence genetically identical.

Morphology: the study of words and their meaningful units; that is, roots, prefixes, suffixes etc., and the rules for forming words out of morphemes.

Motivation: a strong reason to show a particular behaviour; implies that the individual's actions are partly determined in direction and strength by their own inner nature.

Multidisciplinary team: professionals with a variety of different skills and training who work together to provide assessment and/or remediation programs.

Muscular distrophy: a disability that causes a progressive weakness of the skeletal muscles; generally caused by a sex-linked recessive gene.

Mutism: refusal or inability to speak.

N

Narrative recording: a behaviour-observation method that entails continuous and precise description of relevant behaviours and events as they occur.

Natural consequences: what happens naturally as a result of a particular behaviour.

Negative attention: offering disapproval; punishment.

Negative reinforcement: encouraging appropriate behaviour to occur through the withdrawal of aversives when the appropriate behaviour is exhibited. Negative reinforcement increases the future rate and/or probability of the response.

Neonate: a newborn infant.

Nervous breakdown: refers broadly to lowered integration and inability to deal adequately with one's life situation.

Nervous system: system within the body that organises reactions to the environment and changes within the body.

Neurological: pertaining to functioning of the central nervous system.

Neurological examination: examination to determine the presence and extent of organic damage to the nervous system.

Neurology: field concerned with the study of the brain and nervous system, and disorders theory.

Non-categorical: grouping children together without labelling or categorising according to suspected handicaps.

Non-contingent reinforcement: reinforcement that is not related to any specific event.

Non-compliance: being unable or unwilling to accept direction; being unable or unwilling to perform actions or activities except on the person's own terms.

Non-verbal: an inability to communicate verbally.

Non-verbal ability: having skills to perform a task that does not involve using words.

Normal distribution: tendency of most members of a population to cluster around a central point or average with respect to a given trait, with the rest spreading out to the two extremes; a theoretical distribution of probability.

Norm-referenced test: an evaluation that compares an individual's behaviour to the behaviours of others.

Normalisation: the principle of providing disabled persons with environmental conditions that are as close as possible to those of the rest of society.

O

Objectives: statements of the expected behavioural outcomes that will result from instruction. Objectives usually include descriptions of behaviour, conditions for behaviour and criteria.

Object permanence: the realisation that objects continue to exist even though they are out of sight or hidden from view; develops gradually in children between 6 and 18 months of age.

Observation: a process of summarising behaviour by giving examples of time and situation rather than items. During observation, behaviour is looked at without any form of prompting as in testing.

Observable behaviour: behaviour that can be seen, heard or felt.

Observational learning: learning that occurs from watching the behaviour performed by others (models).

Observational recording: methods of data collection used to record aspects of behaviour while it actually occurs, includes event recording, interval recording, time sampling, duration recording and latency recording.

Obsession: repetitive, persistent, preoccupying thoughts about something or someone.

Obsessional language: talking about one topic for extended periods of time while remaining uninterested in others' conversational needs, refusing to change the topic or subject.

Occupational therapy: use of occupational training or activity in psychotherapy. Engaging in activities designed to enhance physical, social, psychological and cognitive development. A major service provided by most rehabilitation centres.

Operant conditioning: form of learning in which a particular response is reinforced and becomes more likely to occur.

Organic retardation: a mental retardation caused by a physiological disorder; for example, Down's syndrome, phenylketonuria, microcephaly.

Osteogenesis imperfecta: a congenital disabilty characterised by defective development of bone tissue, both in quantity and quality.

Outcome: the result or effectiveness of a treatment procedure.

Overcorrection: a procedure used to reduce the occurrence of an inappropriate behaviour. Two forms of overcorrection are:

1 *Restitutional overcorrection*: the offender must restore or correct an environment to its previous condition, and must then improve it beyond its original condition, thereby overcorrecting the environment.

2 *Positive-practice overcorrection*: the offender, having behaved inappropriately, is required to engage in exaggerated practice of appropriate behaviours.

Overlearning: practice beyond the point of mastery in learning a set of materials.

Overextension: the overgeneralisation of a word to inappropriate objects, events or contexts.

Overt behaviour: activities that can be observed by an outsider.

P

Parallel play: playing next to or near another person and being involved in similar activities, but having no noticeable interaction or involvement with them.

Partial reinforcement: reinforcement that occurs at a rate less often than for every correct response or on every trial.

Patterning: working through an activity by modelling correct responses.

Paediatrician: a physician whose speciality is working with and treating infants and young children.

Peer group: social group of equivalent age and status.

Percentile rank: the percentage of scores in a total distribution that a given score equals or exceeds.

Perception: the interpretation of sensory information.

Perceptual motor: the interaction of various channels of perception with motor activity; for example, climbing up stairs is a perceptual motor interaction between visual and gross motor responses.

Performance: a measure of behaviour taken on one occasion.

Performance test: in intelligence testing, a test requiring minimal language; one measuring perceptual skills, spatial abilities, speed etc.

Perinatal: the period of time beginning with birth and extending to the first 3 or 4 weeks of life. Perinatal factors influencing child health include disorders of delivery, infections, prematurity, hypoglycaemia, asphyxia, cardiac irregularities, respiratory difficulties and other factors that may have originated during the prenatal period.

Peripheral vision: the ability to perceive objects outside of the direct line of vision.

Perseveration: persistent continuation of a line of thought or activity once it is started. Clinically, inappropriate repetition.

Perseverative speech: constant repetition of words, phrases, sentences, questions or topics—for self-stimulation, manipulation or as an inappropriate social approach.

Personality: the unique pattern of traits that characterises the individual and determines how others respond to her.

Personal space: the area around an individual that should not be intruded upon, causing discomfort if it is invaded without permission. The amount of personal space required varies both with different people and the set of circumstances at the time.

Petit mal epilepsy: a mild form of epilepsy in which there are momentary losses of consciousness.

Phenylketonuria (PKU): a disorder in the ability to metabolise the amino acid phenylalanine; it is inherited as a recessive trait and causes mental retardation. This mental retardation may be largely mitigated by a special diet.

Phobia: an unreasonable and excessive fear of a specific object, activity or situation that is often not dangerous.

Phoneme: the smallest unit of sound that signals a difference in meaning in a particular language; phonemes are generally divided into consonants and vowels.

Phonetics: the branch of linguistics that analyses and classifies spoken sounds as they are produced by the organs of speech and register on the ear.

Physical assistance: a form of response priming in which the appropriate part or parts are "put through" or physically guided through the proper motion.

Physiotherapist: a trained therapist in the area of motor performance. Services focus on correction, development and prevention of problems of feeding, positioning, ambulation and the development of other gross motor and fine motor skills.

Physical mannerisms: repetitive motor movements such as grimacing, toe-walking, rocking and flapping.

Physical patterning: offering assistance to perform skills or activities by physically moving the body or body parts through the movements required.

Pica: the ingestion of non-food items.

Pictographs: a system of communication using drawings representing words in a pictorial sense, for example Compic.

Pincer grip: coordination of index finger and thumb.

Play therapy: a treatment approach in which play activities are used to establish rapport and communication between child and therapist.

Placebo: a treatment such as a pill identical in all appearances with the one under experimental test, except that it lacks the ingredient being tested.

Placebo effect: an improvement in patients due to psychological factors rather than the medical treatment they are receiving.

Positive attention: offering praise and rewards.

Positive reinforcer: a reward; an event that increases the probability that the response it follows will be made again in similar circumstances.

Postnatal: pertaining to or occurring after birth.

Pragmatics: the rules that govern the use of language by real people in real situations, i.e. the function of language.

Praise: a positive reinforcer using verbal encouragement and congratulation.

Prenatal: pertaining to or occurring before birth.

Prevocational: the basic skills necessary for admission to a vocational program; may include self-help, fine motor and social skills.

Prevalence: the percentage of a population that has a given disorder at some particular time.

Primary cause: cause without which a disorder would not have occurred.

Prognosis: prediction as to the probable course and outcome of a disorder.

Prompt: an added stimulus that increases the probability of a desired response. Prompts are usually faded before the final goal has been achieved.

Prompting: using cues and partial cues to build desired behaviour. Verbal prompting may involve saying a single sound or word to prompt a correct response, while physical prompting involves physical assistance through touch to initiate a motor or self-help skill.

Pronominal reversal: inability of a child to use correct pronouns in speech; tendency for a child to refer to him- or herself as "you" rather than "I".

Prosody: paralinguistic aspects of communication including intonation and stress.

Psychiatrist: medical doctor who specialises in the diagnosis and treatment of mental disorders.

Psychoanalytic model: a model of therapeutic methods developed by Sigmund Freud and his followers:

Psycholinguistics: the study of the psychological aspects of language and its acquisition.

Psychological test: standardised procedure designed to measure a subject's performance on a specified task.

Psychotherapy: treatment of mental disorders by psychological methods.

Psychomotor: involving both psychological and physical activity. Psycho-motor tasks are tests of motor skills that depend on sensory or percep-tual motor coordination.

Puberty: the stage of physical development when reproduction first be-comes possible.

Punishment: the application of unpleasant or discomforting stimulus in order to decrease the probability that the undesirable behaviour it fol-lows will persist.

Q

Qualitative praise: the delivery of praise paired with the rationale or rea-son for its delivery. This reinforces the behaviour and helps the indi-vidual to discriminate about the conditions surrounding the response.

R

Rating scale: device for evaluating oneself or someone else in regard to specific traits.

Ratio schedule of reinforcement: a schedule for the delivery of reinforcers contingent upon the number of correct responses. May be fixed-ratio (FR) schedule or variable-ratio (VR) schedule.

Raw score: the number of responses.

Receptive language: the ability to understand and comprehend the intent and meaning of someone's efforts to communicate.

Recessive gene: a gene that is effective only when paired with an identical gene.

Reciprocity: communicative turn-taking—allowing time for a communica-tive partner to complete their information before beginning to converse, and being aware when another person wants to give input into a conver-sation.

Redirection: changing attention from an inappropriate behaviour to a more appropriate response; encouraging a more appropriate response by redirecting the individual by telling, showing or modelling.

Reflex: a relatively simple, rapid and automatic unlearned response to a stimulus.

Regression: a return to an earlier, simpler and less mature form of behav-iour as a consequence of stress, frustration and failure.

Rehabilitation: use of re-education rather than punishment to overcome behavioural deficits.

Rehearsal: a memory strategy involving the practice of units to be remembered.

Reinforcement: any process that increases the probability of occurrence of a response that is being learned.

Reinforcer: a consequent stimulus that increases or maintains the future rate and/or probability of occurrence of a behaviour.

Reliability: degree to which a test or measuring device produces the same result each time it is used to measure the same thing.

Reliable measurement: refers to the consistency of measurement; occurs when the measuring device remains standard regardless of who uses it and under what conditions.

Repertoire of behaviours: a list of behaviours used frequently by an individual.

Repetitive behaviour: a behaviour that occurs again and again.

Representational systems: non-alphabetic symbol systems that rely primarily on pictures and line drawings.

Residual hearing: the auditory acuity of an individual that remains, without amplification, despite an impairment.

Resistance to change: the inability to tolerate changes in the environment, and the attempts to avoid these.

Respite care: planned or emergency care for a child or adult with a disability, within or outside the family home, which offers relief to the person or family carers for short periods of time. It offers the disabled person opportunities to meet new people and learn new skills.

Response: a directly measurable behaviour.

Response cost: a procedure for the reduction of inappropriate behaviour through withdrawal of specific amounts of reinforcers contingent upon the occurrence of the behaviour.

Response generalisation: unprogrammed changes in similar behaviours when a target behaviour is modified.

Restitution: the rule to restore a situation to the way it was before the occurrence of a behaviour.

Restraint: restricting an individual's movement in some way. In therapy, refers to the physical control used to prevent an inappropriate behaviour from occurring or to reduce the impact of an inappropriate behaviour. May be used to assist the individual to learn to impose self-control.

Retarded: a term used to describe a delay in physical, emotional or intellectual development.

Rett syndrome: a profoundly handicapping neurological disorder that affects only girls. There is a reduction in the rate of head growth and loss of manipulative ability, which is replaced by characteristic hand-wringing movements, usually by the age of 4 years.

Reverse chaining: a process of teaching where the final step of a task is taught first and then other steps are taught consecutively in reverse order. Particularly helpful for teaching self-help skills (also known as backward chaining).

Reward system: a system established to reward certain behaviours while other behaviours do not elicit rewards.

Rewards: objects, events or actions used as a consequence of an appropriate behaviour in order to encourage further occurrence of the behaviour —it must, therefore, be highly individually motivating.

Rigid behaviour: the apparent need to perform activities in the same way each time they are performed; the inability to accept change in the environment.

Ritalin: a central nervous system stimulant often used to treat hyperactivity in children.

Ritual: a series of actions compulsively performed under certain circumstances, the non-performance of which leads to tension and anxiety.

Role playing: acting out the behaviour the individual believes is expected of a certain role, in a hypothetical and staged situation.

Rote learning: learning of verbal sequences with little attention to meaning.

Routine: a more or less mechanical or unvarying performance of certain acts or duties.

S

Sample: a group from a population selected for special study that is truly representative of that population.

Satiation: the state that occurs when a reinforcer has been presented to the point that it is no longer effective in increasing or maintaining behaviour; the opposite of deprivation.

Schedule of reinforcement: the specific pattern of partial reinforcement.

Schizophrenia: a group of disorders marked by major dysfunction of thinking, emotion and behaviour. Disturbances in thinking take the form of illogicality, faulty associative inferences and delusional beliefs. Perception is also disturbed with hallucinations (auditory, visual and tactile) common. Social relationships are minimal and withdrawal from others is a characteristic pattern.

Screening: the process of sorting out from a particular population those children who may have problems and need further diagnostic testing.

Secondary reinforcer: reinforcement provided by a stimulus that has gained value by being associated with a primary reinforcing stimulus.

Self-care skills: skills of looking after oneself: these include feeding, toileting, bathing, dressing and independent travel.

Self-esteem: feeling of personal worth.

Self-injurious behaviour: behaviour that is characterised by deliberately hurting oneself, usually by hitting, biting, punching etc. It may be a reaction to intrusion, anger or frustration, a form of self-stimulation or a need for sensory stimulation.

Semantic Pragmatic Disorder: Communication disorder involving understanding and use of meaning in language and problems communicating functionally.

Sensorimotor: a term applied to the combination of the input of sense organs and the output of motor activity. The motor activity reflects what is happening to the sensory organs, such as the visual, auditory, tactile and kinesthetic sensations.

Sensory: pertaining to the senses.

Separation anxiety: crying, fretting and discomfort reflective of a child's unhappiness when separated from a familiar adult (typically a parent or carer) to whom the child is attached and dependent.

Shaping: the process of reinforcing closer and closer approximations to a desired response.

Siblings: offspring of the same parents.

Signing: a form of communication using gestures, hand and finger movements; usually a standardised method is used.

Social cognition: the individual's understanding of the social world, of other people and of personal relations with them.

Social motivation: the desire to interact with others.

Social reinforcer: a category of secondary reinforcers that includes facial expressions, proximity, contact, privileges, words and phrases.

Social skills: ability to relate to others and to the environment.

Socialisation: a child's acquisition through experience of the values and habits of the culture.

Sorting: discrimination and separation according to differences.

Special school: specific schools for children with different disabilities who are unable to be placed in a regular school.

Specific language disorder: a term applied to individuals with any language deficit—oral, visual or auditory.

Speech pathologist: trained specialist who works with students with articulation or language delay as well as children with more serious speech disorders or in any form of communication disorder.

Splinter skills: highly specific isolated skills that are developed to satisfy demands lying beyond a child's regular skill development.

Standardised test: tests that are administered in a specifically described standard way, scored in a particular way and then compared with the performance of a standard group.

Stereotype: expectations and opinions about large groups of people without any regard for individual differences.

Stimuli: information that can be received by the senses or any antecedent condition or cause of behaviour.

Successive approximations: the process of gradually increasing expectations for a child to display behaviours that are more like a desired target behaviour; used in shaping behaviours not previously a part of the child's behaviour pattern.

Symbol: image, word, object or activity that is used to represent something else; abstract representation of a word or concept.

Symptom: an observable manifestation of a physical or mental disorder.

Syndrome: a cluster or pattern of symptoms that characterise a specific disorder.

Syntax: the rules by which words may be combined into phrases and sentences. Grammar is the most familiar example.

Systematic desensitisation: a form of behaviour therapy devised by J. Wolpe and based on the principle of counter conditioning. An individual in a state of relaxation learns to cope with situations or objects previously feared.

T

Tactile: the sense of touch.

Tactile defensiveness: the inability to tolerate touch by a person, object, surface or texture.

Tantrum: uncontrolled expression of anger or frustration. May involve screaming, crying, aggression and destruction, self-abuse or physical lack of control.

Target behaviour: the terminal objective or final desired behaviour that is the goal of shaping when using behavioural objectives. Also refers to the negative behaviour to be modified in a behaviour-modification program.

Task analysis: the process of breaking down a complex behaviour into its component parts.

Telegraphic speech: term used to describe early sentences that tend to resemble telegrams—articles, prepositions and conjunctions are frequently omitted while nouns and verbs are overused.

Temperament: a very general aspect of personality typically associated with characteristic mood, level of activity, adaptability. Increasingly, a constitutional factor is thought to underlie it.

Time out: reducing inappropriate behaviour by denying the individual access, for a fixed period of time, to the opportunity to receive reinforcement.

Time-sampling: an observational recording system in which an observation period is divided into equal intervals; the target behaviour is observed at the end of each interval.

Token economy: a reinforcement technique in which individuals are rewarded for socially constructive behaviour with tokens that can then be exchanged for desired material goods, services or privileges.

Token reinforcer: a symbol or object that can be exchanged at a later time for a "back-up" reinforcer—an item or activity; for example, money is a token. The extent to which tokens are reinforcing depends on the individual's experience and on the "back-up" items available.

Total communication: a philosophy in teaching communication that includes using aural, manual and oral methods to ensure effective communication.

Trait: characteristic of individual that can be observed or measured.

Trial and error learning: complex operant or instrumental learning in which an individual selects the correct response in a particular situation by eliminating erroneous responses.

Trisomy 21: a condition of having three rather than two of the 21st chromosomes; the cause of Down's syndrome.

Tuberous sclerosis: disease causing tumours within the brain; progressive mental deterioration and epileptic seizures.

U

Unconditioned stimulus (US): a stimulus that produces a consistent response at the onset of training.

Unconditioned response (UR): a response elicited by the unconditioned stimulus without special training.

Unconscious: a general term for classes of activities that are not open to conscious awareness.

Unstructured: situations where patterning is not definite, but is vague, ambiguous or capable of different interpretations.

Utterance: something that is said or produced orally.

V

Validity: the extent to which test scores measure what they are intended to measure.

Variable: a measurable entity that can vary in the values it takes.

Verbal expression: the ability to express ideas verbally.

Verbal IQ: intelligence test scores derived from tests measuring the use of language, reasoning, vocabulary, general knowledge, comprehension etc.

Visual: perceived through sight.

Visual discrimination: the ability to discern similarities and differences visually.

Visual-motor: the ability to relate visual stimuli to motor responses in an appropriate way.

Visual-motor coordination: the ability to coordinate vision with the movements of the body or parts of the body.

Visual perception: the identification, organisation and interpretation of sensory data received by the individual through the eyes.

Vitamin therapy: the use of vitamins to stabilise behaviour in some overactive children.

Vocal: the ability to use sounds that may or may not be used as a form of communication.

Vocalisation: sounds made using the vocal chords.

Vocational: skill training for work placement.

W

WAIS (Wechsler Adult Intelligence Scale): an individual intelligence test developed by David Wechsler for adults. Provides for verbal performance and composite IQ scores.

Wechsler scales: *see* WAIS and WISC.

Williams syndrome: a syndrome of infantile hyper-calcaemia (elevated blood-calcium levels), heart abnormalities and a characteristic facial appearance. As yet, the cause of the syndrome is unknown.

WISC (Wechsler Intelligence Scale for Children): a test like the WAIS, developed by David Wechsler for children. Provides for verbal performance and composite IQ scores.

Withdrawal: a defensive response to stress in which the person is profoundly listless and indifferent, and avoids contact with others.

Word association test: a test, sometimes used for personality diagnosis, in which a person gives the first word that comes to mind in response to a series of stimulus words spoken by the examiner.

Word attack skills: skills enabling the analysis of unfamiliar words by syllables and phonic elements to arrive at their correct pronunciation.

Word order: the order in which words are spoken in a sentence.

X

X axis (abscissa): the horizontal axis on a graph; usually represents the independent variable.

X chromosome: a sex-determining chromosome; all female gametes contain X chromosomes, and if the fertilised ovum has also received an X chromosome from the male, offspring will be female.

XYY syndrome: a chromosomal anomaly in males—the presence of an extra Y chromosome; possibly related to impulsive behaviour.

Y

Y axis (ordinate): the vertical axis on a graph; usually represents the dependent variable.

Y chromosome: a sex-determining chromosome found in half of the total number of male gametes; uniting with the X chromosome always provided by female gametes produces male offspring.

Z

Zygote: a fertilised egg cell formed by the union of male and female gametes.

Index